CREATIVE @ WORK

Dear Ate Elizabeth,

Thank you so much for helping make this childhood dream a reality. I really appreciate all your support ♡

Hope we can hangout soon!

Love,

Andrea Liu

CREATIVE @ WORK

Andrea R. Lirio

NEW DEGREE PRESS

COPYRIGHT © 2021 ANDREA R. LIRIO

CREATIVE @ WORK

ISBN

978-1-63676-715-4   *Paperback*

978-1-63730-052-7   *Kindle Ebook*

978-1-63730-154-8   *Digital Ebook*

Thank you for believing in me Mom & Dad.

This book is for you.

CONTENTS

Creativity.
A scary thought.
   A splash on the page,
   A forgotten idea.
Because when I think about it ...
I wonder;
Where would we be without it?

Creativity is in everything, creativity is everywhere.
Creativity is art.
Creativity has no bounds.

You are creativity, creativity is you.
Embrace, learn, and believe you too

are creative.

INTRODUCTION

———

This book is about creators and artists.

But it starts with numbers.

Students are lining up to grab their undergraduate business degrees. Today, business is one of the most popular majors, with 386,201 business majors per year in the US.[1] This number doesn't even include the many Liberal Arts students looking to pursue a career in business after college. In the US, 192,184 people with an undergraduate degree go on to pursue their MBAs every year.[2]

Worldwide, 582 million entrepreneurs are working on their businesses,[3] and 62 percent of adults in the US believe entrepre-

———

1   Erin Duffin, "Number of Bachelor's Degrees Earned in the United States in 2017/18," *Statista*, November 30, 2020.

2   Ibid.

3   Donna Kelley, "The 582 Million Entrepreneurs in the World Are Not Created Equal," *The Hill*, March 12, 2017.

neurship is a good career path.[4] The number of entrepreneurs is ever-increasing, with more people hoping to find flexibility in their day-to-day life and the ambition to solve the world's problems.

But despite its popularity, we have an incomplete view of entrepreneurship. Typically, entrepreneurship is defined as the following:

en·tre·pre·neur·ship
/ˌäntrəprəˈnərˌship/

noun

the activity of setting up a business or businesses, taking on financial risks in the hope of profit.

ex. "the new business opportunities have encouraged entrepreneurship on a grand scale."[5]

I also sat down with over forty college students and engaged in community forums about the view on business and entrepreneurship. The first words that came to their minds were: corporations, profit, finance, investing, numbers, computer science, data, math, and management.

But entrepreneurship, to me, is like art. Entrepreneurs, like artists, are unwilling to conform, and they create what they envision.

---

4   Damien O'Brien and Brian Fitzgerald, "Digital Copyright Law in a YouTube World," *Internet Law Bulletin* 9, no. 6 (2007): 71-115.

5   Oxford Languages, Version 12.4., s.v. "Entrepreneurship," Oxford University Press, 2021.

Sitting at our wooden school desks, my best friend Mona and I wrote short story after short story in our composition notebooks. Like many excited and creative fourth graders, we loved imagining an entirely new fictional world. We thought we were going to become the world's next best authors. We loved every second of brainstorming new content and sharing it with our friends and family. But like many things, we let go of our dreams to become young adult novelists and left our notebooks in the box at the back of our closets. I've often looked back at my creations in that class. What would have happened today if we had decided to pursue it? My young dream of becoming a novelist died with my socialized belief that being creative wouldn't lead to success.

Instead, I set my sights on business, a field that seemed more practical. What I found, though, is that my entrepreneurial pursuits are unexpectedly driven by the creativity nurtured by my childhood dream of becoming an author.

Most people believe only a select few have creative ability when, in reality, we're all born creative. In a NASA study that measured creativity over time from preschool to high school, it was found that we're all born with immense creative talent but lose creativity over time.[6]

School, work, and adult life wears down our minds to see creative goals as unproductive and unnecessary.

Many college students end up conforming and following what they perceive to be the correct path to success in business. All

---

6   *TEDx Talks*, "TEDx Tucson George Lan the Failure of Success," February 16, 2011. video, 13:06.

they can talk about is getting an analyst or associate role at a big consulting firm. Computer science majors gush about getting internships at the biggest names in Silicon Valley, and Finance and Economics majors fight for the top investment banking roles. They become obsessed with making "big money" in business. As one of my friends put it, "College students these days are so quick to sell out."

We're always told one path in business: make a profit above all else. Still, so rarely do people highlight the creativity behind building a successful product or project. While roles in consulting, technology, and finance are notable, they only make up a part of all the possible business opportunities in the world. I believe the common perception forgets my favorite part of business: the art of creating and having the imagination and ability to execute on an idea. For me, being an entrepreneur is the ultimate creative experience. To me, entrepreneurship is a form of art.

Being an entrepreneur doesn't mean you necessarily have to start a business. Entrepreneurship is far more than being a business owner. It's a perspective. Like artists, entrepreneurs are creative non-conformists with grit and determination, looking to solve today's problems.

We need to think of creatives less as a department in the workplace or a skill that artists have. Instead, we need to see creativity in its many forms.

Consider award-winning artists like Jon Favreau, Taylor Swift, and Mindy Kaling. While it may not seem like it at first, they are all full-fledged entrepreneurs. They've not only created something beautiful for movies, music, and television, but they've also developed technology to enhance their work and have set the stage for future artists to join and innovate. There's a parallel between these artists and entrepreneurs such as Steve Jobs, Mark Zuckerberg, and Jeff Bezos. They are all creative thinkers who created companies by finding a problem and addressing it.

This book is essential for businesspeople, entrepreneurs, and students thinking about what they want to do. This book will look at artists, examine how creativity works, and dive into what makes a creative businessperson. Creative thinkers are all around us, from creating cupcake stores to founding the world's largest marketplaces. Business is more than profit, and entrepreneurship is art.

PART 1

THE ART OF CREATIVITY

1.

THE ENTREPRENEURIAL MINDSET

W hat do you think is the difference between business and entrepreneurship?

I sat down with more than forty students and engaged in student forums to understand college students' overall perspectives on business. The first ideas that came to mind were often traditional corporate roles, working to make a profit, and strong management. Similarly enough, today, business is defined as "organized efforts and activities of individuals to produce and sell goods and services for profit."[7]

When I asked students about entrepreneurship, their perspectives shifted. To them, entrepreneurship was the pursuit of creating new value. They noted that it was a field with high risk and potential for high reward. In addition, they argued that entrepreneurship is the stepping stone to joining the world

---

7   Adam Hayes, "What is A Business," *Investopedia*, July 4, 2020.

of business. As they saw it, the most famous businesspeople once started with lean and innovative startups.

Despite these positive connotations with entrepreneurship, students from the world's top universities and colleges, interested in pursuing business, often target roles in the trifecta—consulting, finance, and technology. In 2017, fifty percent of Harvard University's graduates went into one of the three industries.[8] These roles don't even begin to describe the array of opportunities in the world of business and entrepreneurship.

Most of our school systems and workplaces don't support the creative mindset. With rigid hours, clear structure, productivity-run goals, there is little emphasis on arts and exploration. College prepares students to become young professionals. Even when art and creativity are part of the curriculum, they're the first to go when the school or organization faces budget cuts. "People generally think that the arts are nice and culturally significant and all that, but most people don't have much of a vision of why the arts are really important in people's personal, civic, and professional lives," Professor David Perkins, a founding member of Project Zero said. "From my point of view, engagement with art and the creating of art are opportunities for students to learn to think in one or another medium. After all, thinking in one or another medium is what we have to do every day as we engage the complexities of contemporary life."[9]

8   Thomas Franck, "Post-Harvard Plans," *The Harvard Crimson*, 2017.

9   Mary Tamer, "On the Chopping Block, Again," *Harvard ED*, Summer 2009.

Creativity is something we all take for granted. It's often given a bad rap when we think of useful life skills, and it's mostly due to society's conception and bias that art—like paintings, sculptures, and music—isn't practical. Instead, we like to focus on tangible things like money and belongings, and we reward those who are the most productive or achieve the most. Today, students view business as a respectable career path to become their own boss and make money.

But business is far more than that; it requires creativity. Creativity is "the use of the imagination or original ideas, especially in the production of an artistic work."[10] And in a 2020 study by the World Economic Forum, creativity will become one of the top three skills workers will need. The definition of creativity is ever-changing, according to France's Sciences Pro Professor and bestselling author Rahaf Harfoush: "We're no longer artists praying for divine inspiration; we're productive creatives who are contributing to economics and markets that were built on the tenets of productivity."[11] It's often overlooked, but creativity plays a crucial role in any business endeavor. The question is, how did we end up where we are today? While students are rushing to get their business degrees—the top undergraduate and graduate degree in the country—we still forget to teach the importance of creativity in every profession.

We need to teach our kids to be entrepreneurs. I don't mean we need to tell every child to start their own business and

---

10   Oxford Languages, Version 12.4., s.v. "Creativity," Oxford University Press, 2021.

11   Scott Belskey, "Creativity Will Be Key To Competing Against AI In The Future Workforce-Here's How," *World Economic Forum*, November 10, 2020.

become CEOs and founders when they grow up. I mean we need to instill the entrepreneurial mindset of creative thinking.

Recognize opportunities, take initiative to pursue them, and execute those ideas.

According to the Network for Teaching Entrepreneurship (NFTE), these are key aspects of the entrepreneurial mindset:[12]

- Critical Thinking

- Flexibility & Adaptability

- Communication & Collaboration

- Comfort with Risk

- Initiative & Self Reliance

- Future Orientation

- Opportunity Recognition

- Creativity & Innovation

Like artists, entrepreneurs are creative non-conformists with grit and determination, looking to solve today's problems.

I witnessed this first-hand from my aunt.

---

12   "Entrepreneurial Mindset ," NFTE, accessed February 16, 2021.

She was twenty-one and in college when she had her first child, and she still pursued an education through graduate school, getting both her MBA and JD. There, she had her second child, and with her workload and need to care for her children, she faced a somewhat common but dire situation: she needed a caregiver. It was her creative solution to a unique but widespread problem that led to the creation of Care.com.

Her ability to take a simple problem in her own life and create, fund, scale, and bring a company public has always inspired me. Her work was always mission-driven, which drove me to pursue a career in social entrepreneurship. She knew that the only way to make the world a better, more welcoming place was envisioning it as such and creating a path toward that reality. To this day, she continues to teach me about pursuing creative and purpose-driven projects. Creating Care. com wasn't easy; she and many other entrepreneurs had to be scrappy. They needed to figure out how to raise money for their project and build a strong and passionate team. And once they had the resources, they needed to execute the plan and convince people to use their platform.

The truth is creativity takes a lot of practice, hard work, and discipline. While we're all born inherently creative, we still need to put our creative brains to work, like working out any muscle. These are all things we can learn to achieve and do. So, instead of seeing business as a profit-seeking entity, look at it as a playground to explore your most creative self.

Think of entrepreneurship as the pursuit of problem-solving, innovation, and creative thinking. You don't necessarily have to start your own business to be an entrepreneur, but there are key aspects in every entrepreneur and creator that are crucial in every endeavor.

To me, business through entrepreneurship is a form of art and the ultimate form of creativity. The creative ideas you come up with are puzzle pieces to the final product. It requires the right skills, ambition, drive, team, dedication, and support to make the puzzle into a masterpiece.

Behind every successful businessperson, we'll find a story about how they creatively found a way to make their idea into a reality, whether that be creative problem solving, storytelling, building a strong team or making tough decisions. All of these situations require creativity and the ability to think outside the box.

2.

WHAT IS CREATIVITY?

BREAKING IT DOWN

cre·a·tiv·i·ty
/ˌkrēāˈtivədē/

noun

the use of the imagination or original ideas,
especially in the production of an artistic work.

ex. "firms are keen to encourage creativity"[13]

M ost commonly, we view artists as creative, and creativity is often matched with creating sculptures or paintings to writing poetry or music.

---

13   Oxford Languages, Version 12.4., s.v. "Creativity," Oxford University Press, 2021.

But in a broader sense, creativity can come in many different forms. One could say doctors are creative when they diagnose diseases, scientists are creative when they come up with new theories, and entrepreneurs are creative when they create new products.[14]

So, we need to come to a clear understanding of what creativity is and how we will define it for the purpose of this book.

Creativity is often seen to have two or three major components. According to the American Psychological Association, creativity includes originality and functionality.[15] Creative ideas are usually different, new, or innovative; they are ideas that actually work and possess some form of usefulness. So, not only do creative ideas need to be new and innovative, but they also have to be useful. This definition, in and of itself, also makes clear why people are so adamant that they aren't creative. The standard seems almost too high for anyone to say they are creative. So, we need to break it down further, to make it a more accessible reality for more people.

Within creativity, experts suggest there are four different types:[16]

1. "Mini-c" creativity

2. "Little-c" creativity

---

14   Mitch Resnick, "4 Myths About Creativity," *Edutopia*, November 20, 2017.

15   Amy Novotney, "The Science Of Creativity," *APA*, January 2009.

16   James Kaufman and Ronald Beghetto, "Beyond Big And Little: The Four C Model Of Creativity," *Sage Journals* 13, no. 1(2009): 1-12.

3. "Pro-c" creativity

4. "Big-c" creativity.

"Mini-c" creativity involves personal, meaningful interpretations of experiences, actions, and events. In other words, we have new and creative experiences every day as individuals, but they're not necessarily revolutionary. For example, when I was in elementary school and used to bake with Betty Crocker mixes at home, I was completing the work and it was something new and also meaningful for me, especially as I was growing up. Impactful moments of new experience are seen as a key form of creativity.

"Little-c" creativity involves everyday thinking and problem-solving. This type of creativity helps people adapt to the ever-changing environment and address common problems. For example, creating a new recipe instead of using a mix or teaching my dog a new trick falls under "little-c." They're not often seen as inherently creative, but they are because they require a form of outside of the box thinking day-to-day.

"Pro-c" creativity takes place among professionals. At this point, they've had a lot of experience and refinement in their respective field and know how to support themselves by doing what they love. Often times, professionals are skilled in a particular field, but they don't necessarily "achieve eminence for their works."[17] For example, if I continued to pursue my love for baking and opened my own bakery, I would fall into the category of "pro-c," which means I'm able to support myself

---

17 James Kaufman and Ronald Beghetto, "Beyond Big And Little: The Four C Model Of Creativity," *Sage Journals* 13, no. 1(2009): 1-12.

and more people are able to appreciate my work and creation. The mere fact that other people are able to appreciate it and make use of it, makes that form of creativity, "pro-c."

"Big-c" creativity involves the creatives that go down in history books. It includes creating works and ideas that are considered the greatest in their field. This type of creativity often leads to world-changing creations and innovations. Think of Albert Einstein, Chef Gordon Ramsey, Louis Armstrong, Elon Musk, Amanda Gorman, Whitney Houston, John Williams, and Picasso. They're known for their extraordinary work that impacted our society today which will be remembered and passed down for generations.

In the end, we're all creative; it just depends on the type of creativity that you're referring to. You could also look at it this way: having new ideas without acting on them is imaginative but not necessarily creative.

And while having an imaginative mindset is important in entrepreneurship—from coming up with new products to finding new ways to reach customers—it's not enough to succeed. Imagine there are two separate writers. There's one writer who tells you about a great story they want to write but doesn't write it. The other writer has a similar idea and goes for it and starts writing. We'd probably say the second person is a great creative artist because they produced amazing work. For the first person, though, we can't say the same even though they came up with the same idea. There's a huge difference between being a talker and a creator. Many people have amazing ideas, which makes them super imaginative but not everyone is creative, in terms of actually executing on the project.

Before we jump to conclusions and claim that we're not creative, we need to understand that creativity comes in different forms. We don't need to be the next Picasso to be creative. Instead, we need to take a step back and view our small moments as creative stepping stones and success points.

SCIENCE OF CREATIVITY

"Creativity is absolutely for everyone. I firmly believe this. I think if you're the driest accountant with the plastic pocket pen protector, it's in how you interact with the world. There's artistry in everything that we do."

                                                            - RAINN WILSON

The science of creativity is a continuously evolving concept, and the scientific community has yet to reach a consensus. What we currently understand is that creativity is a mix of a person's genetics and experience. Creativity is just a combination of distinct mental processes.

In the past, scientists thought creativity came from only one hemisphere of the brain: the right side.[18] From more recent studies, however, we now know the brain is made up of complex neural networks that spark creativity. According to psychologist John R. Hayes, creativity is "the potential of persons to produce creative works whether or not they have

---

18   John R. Hayes, "Cognitive Process In Creativity," *Handbook Of Creativity*, (1989): 135-145.

produced any work as yet."[19] And creativity is used as a term to describe a process of a lot of different kinds of thinking.

To harness our creativity, we need to understand how our brains work. Psychologists like to explain it in terms of the three main brain networks:

1. Executive Attention Network

2. Default Mode Network

3. Salience Brain Network

The **Executive Attention Network** is the area of the brain that integrates a lot of information that comes in.[20] It serves to hold information in your working memory and helps you when you're creating something. Think of it as a laser beam. The network is active when you're concentrating on something challenging or in "complex problem solving and reasoning that puts heavy demands on working memory."[21] For example, this area of the brain helps the best improvisation artists focus. When they're creating, the brain recognizes that the first few iterations will not be as strong. So, you hold information on how you did something before and continue to improve upon it until you reach a strong creation.

---

19   Mitch Resnick, "4 Myths About Creativity," *Edutopia*, November 20, 2017.

20   *Wheeler Centre*, "David Eagleman: The Creative Brain," May 28, 2018, video, 1:04:50.

21   *Wheeler Centre*, "David Eagleman: The Creative Brain," May 28, 2018, video, 1:04:50.

The **Default Mode Network** (aka the Imaginative Network) is the area of your brain that daydreams and imagines the future. This part of the brain focuses on compassion and understanding the world outside of your own perspective. *Scientific American* notes that the Default Network is involved in "constructing dynamic mental simulations based on personal past experiences used during remembering, thinking about the future, and generally when imaginative alternative perspectives and scenarios are present."[22]

Lastly, the **Salience Brain Network** focuses on what is most interesting to us. Think of it as a tag machine that marks every time something is interesting or not. With every tag, the brain knows whether or not to feed it to the Executive of Imaginative Network to explore more. It "monitors both external events and the internal stream of consciousness and flexibly passes the baton to whatever information is most salient to solving the task at hand."[23]

So, there isn't one area wholly responsible for creativity. In fact, all the areas working together are key to becoming your most creative self. Creativity involves the interaction of all three networks. We're captivated, mindful, imaginative, and motivated to engage in the creative endeavor.

There's another study psychologists bring to attention when studying creativity: understanding the importance of bending, breaking, and blending.[24]

---

22 Ibid.

23 Ibid.

24 Anthony Brandt and David Eagleman, "How Your Brain Takes Good Ideas and Makes Them Better," *Psychology Today*, October 10, 2017.

According to psychologist David Eagleman, creative opportunity has gone up because there's more resources and information than ever to work with in the world. What we create often has a lot to do with what we absorb. Instead of thinking of creativity as brand-new ideas, think of it as an idea that has a second life. Like many artists and entrepreneurs have shared, Eagleman notes that new ideas are just a connection between old ones.[25]

In our brain, we go through three processes to come up with new ideas. We bend, break, and blend—the three Bs.

Bending is when you modify an idea. For example, artists sometimes physically bend a project to create a new work of art, and entrepreneurs modify a step in the process to make something different.

Breaking is when you take the entire thing apart. For example, artists may dismantle a sculpture to understand how it was put together, and entrepreneurs break down an entire product to understand how it functions.

Blending is when you combine two or more ideas/concepts. For example, some artists have quite literally mixed two colors to find new ones, and entrepreneurs take ideas from two separate products and combine them into one.

---

25   Ibid.

The three Bs are a way of "capturing the brain operations that underlie innovative thinking."[26] Bending, breaking and blending highlight the brain's ability to think outside the box.

We've come to understand that our brains use a lot of different pathways to communicate and come up with new ideas. Creativity depends on the cooperation of the three main networks and the ability to operate the three Bs. Our brain works best when it observes and reacts to things around us; the best creators cover the spectrum.

"The thing about any sort of creative
act is that you never know what's
going to stick and what will actually
make a difference in your society."[27]

- DAVID EAGLEMAN

So, it's our job to keep testing and iterating and figure out what will stick.

---

26 Anthony Brandt and David Eagleman, "How Your Brain Takes Good Ideas and Makes Them Better," *Psychology Today*, October 10, 2017.

27 *Wheeler Centre*, "David Eagleman: The Creative Brain," May 28, 2018, video, 1:04:50.

3.

FIRST THINGS FIRST: YOU DON'T HAVE TO BE A 'GENIUS'

———

gen·ius
/ˈjēnyəs/

noun

exceptional intellectual or creative power or other natural ability.

ex. "she was a teacher of genius"

a person who is exceptionally intelligent or creative, either generally or in some particular respect.

ex. "one of the great musical geniuses of the twentieth century"[28]

———

28 Oxford Languages, Version 12.4., s.v. "Genius," Oxford University Press, 2021.

So often, we look at creative people as geniuses which makes it difficult to believe we can be creative too. No matter what people say, you don't have to be a genius to do great things. What I've noticed is most people don't think they are creative because they compare themselves with the greats in history, also known as "Big-C" creativity. We often judge ourselves because we can't come up with amazing new innovations or unique ideas right away that make a huge impact on society.

We all know the classic young genius founder story.

Mark Zuckerberg dropped out of Harvard University during his sophomore year to found and grow Facebook, which is now the most well-known and powerful social media and social networking site in the world.[29]

Facebook went live in 2004 and reached 1 million users by the end of the year.[30] The current Chairman and CEO of Facebook is praised for creating the site and being a computer science genius at only nineteen. At twenty-three, Zuckerberg became a self-made billionaire, the youngest in history at the time, in 2008.[31]

Today, he continues to lead Facebook and is known for his role in acquiring even more social media platforms and starting a

---

29 Evan Tarver, "Mark Zuckerberg Success Story: Net Worth, Education, and Influence," *Investopedia*, January 31, 2020.

30 "Company Info," About Facebook, accessed January 29, 2021.

31 Kathleen Elkins and Taylor Rogers, "How Old 14 of the World's Richest People Were When They First Became Billionaires," *Business Insider*, August 10, 2020.

new generation of media. Almost anyone you meet will know the story of the young drop-out genius. On many occasions, I've sat down with my own family members who talk about who the next Zuckerberg will be in the world and what that person will spearhead. Through our many discussions, I noticed that we have a very interesting mindset when it comes to thinking about business. For one, we think there's a race to be the youngest billionaire or youngest businessperson. In addition to being the youngest, you could compete for other medals like who would achieve the most, be the most well-known, or make the most money. Lastly, you could compete for who would come up with the best idea.

For some reason, as a society, we've put together an Olympics of sorts when it comes to creating in the business world. Not only are we focused on collecting as many medals as we can, we have this mindset that you have to be a genius to come up with an idea that is even worthy of a so-called prize. This is a result of well-known stories of Mark Zuckerberg, Bill Gates, Michael Dell, or Steve Jobs, who have all dropped out and led the forefront in successful companies.

Joining today's business world and being the next Zuckerberg seems so unattainable because it seems like it's only for a few people to achieve that sort of success. While I'm not saying you'll be the next self-made billionaire or lead a Fortune 500 Company, I believe we can all be creative, like many notable businesspeople and artists who come up with solutions to today's problems no matter the scale. Instead of looking at productivity and what someone is able to do, we need to focus on how they were able to do it so we can apply what they've done to future work and continue to challenge and innovate.

As Steve Jobs so aptly put it, "Life can be much broader once you discover one simple fact, and that is: Everything around you that you call life, was made up by people that were no smarter than you."[32]

Remember, creativity is infinite. Instead of focusing on how you're incapable of following other innovators, creators, and artists, you have to remember you don't have to be a genius to be creative. Creativity can be learned and strengthened. In fact, according to Dr. George Land and Dr. Beth Jarman, both of whom conducted a study at NASA, most of us are born at genius level.[33]

In a study on creativity by NASA, researchers found that 98 percent of preschoolers, of the 1,600 children tested were considered creative geniuses. They retested the same children at ten years, and again at fifteen years of age.[34]

The test results:

- 98 percent in preschool

- 30 percent in grade school

- 12 percent in high school

- Less than 2 percent in 280,000 adults

---

32   "A Quote by Steve Jobs," Goodreads, accessed January 29, 2021.

33   "Study Shows We are Born Creative Geniuses but the 'Education' System Dumbs Us Down," Twenty One Toys, accessed January 29, 2021.

34   *Ted X Talks*, "TEDx Tucson George Lan the Failure of Success," February 16, 2011, video, 13:06.

"What we have concluded," wrote Land, "is that non-creative behavior is learned."[35]

We often feel we're not creative enough, and that's because we've been taught through a less creative stream. We need to flip that switch and recognize that we can reteach ourselves and see the world with open eyes like we did as kids.

Take founder and CEO of Insomnia Cookies, Seth Berkowitz, for example. While in his college dorm room, he created a brand beloved by college students across the nation. Trust me, once you have his cookies, you'll be ordering them every late study night. I'm guilty of it. And in case you're still looking for medal-worthy work, it's a company worth $500 million by just selling cookies.[8]

A student at the Wharton School of the University of Pennsylvania at the time, Berkowitz noticed that his peers weren't really into startups. According to Berkowitz, everyone wanted to work at Goldman Sachs or a big bank, but after interning at an investment banking firm, he just realized it wasn't for him. He wasn't entirely sure what that meant and what he would do. One thing he did know was he loved cookies and sweet treats. And he noticed that a lot of other students liked them too, especially late at night.[36]

That was the spark. He spent long hours toiling over recipes alone in his dorm. He put everything into making the best

---

35 Rajat Bhageria, "An Interview With Seth Berkowitz | How the Founder of Insomnia has Revolutionized The College Experience Armed Only With Cookies," *HuffPost*, February 17, 2015.

36 Ibid.

cookies and started by giving samples away at Locust Walk. Everybody loved them. They became a success, and he figured out that people were willing to pay for his product, especially if he was able to deliver them. He noticed there weren't many options to order late at night. That's when he was able to create the revolutionary business model to make Insomnia unique. He would cater specifically to students and deliver at odd hours in the night.

After a few years experimenting in his dorm, he went on to get FDA approval and set up his first retail store in New York. He got a few investors to believe in his idea by taking a savvy and less glamorous marketing approach; he started giving away free samples, and went around different campuses convincing students to just try his cookies. Word spread fast. He took advantage of student social media and made his brand known.

While Berkowitz isn't acclaimed like Zuckerberg or Gates, it's interesting to note that he took the road less traveled.

Early on, Berkowitz understood that business doesn't just consist of finance, investment banking, and consulting. Besides that, Berkowitz knew creativity is at the helm of success in any business venture, no matter the role. He teaches us the importance of believing in your venture and passion even if you don't classify yourself as a "genius." Anyone can be creative, and your creation can come from anything and start anywhere—even just baking cookies for college students.

We need creative confidence, the belief that you can do it and can master the art of creativity. The truth is success is largely a numbers game; we need to experience enough failure to finally create a gem. So don't be too impatient with yourself. And remember, as author James Clear reminds us, "Even people of considerable talent rarely produce incredible work before decades of practice."[37]

We have to demystify the idea that one has to be a Zuckerberg or Gates and embrace that you, too, can succeed in a creative venture. Creativity shouldn't be a competition. It should be an opportunity for exploration and growth.

---

37 James Clear, "Breaking Through Mental Blocks, Uncover Your Creative Genius, and Make Brilliance a Habit," *Mastering Creativity 1*, (2014): 36.

PART 2

GET IN, WE'RE GOING TO CREATE

4.

THE ART OF BEING DISRUPTIVE

"Don't be scared if you don't do things in the right order, or if you don't do some things at all," actress, producer, and author Mindy Kaling pronounced to Dartmouth College graduates during her commencement speech.[38]

Kaling's thoughts encapsulate what I like to call the "disruptive creator mindset." This term is inspired by the theory of disruptive innovation coined by Harvard Business School professor Clayton Christensen. Christensen's theory explains that "disruptive innovation refers to a new development that dramatically changes the way a structure or industry functions."[39] Think of the internet; it dramatically changed the world of business by forcing companies to either adapt or lose.

---

38 *Dartmouth*, "Dartmouth's 2018 Commencement Address by Mindy Kaling '01," June 10, 2018, video, 17:02.

39 Alexandra Twin, "Disruptive Innovation," *Investopedia*, March 8, 2017.

But rather than altering an industry, a disruptive creator is a person who interrupts their own traditional journey to pursue something out of the box; they're not concerned with doing things in a particular order.

Take Kaling herself; she is a non-conforming disruptive creator. When there wasn't a place for her in Hollywood, she decided to make one by creating TV shows and films that would represent her. Today, Kaling is best known for writing and acting on *The Office*, developing and producing *The Mindy Project*, voice acting in *Inside Out*, and working alongside Oprah and Reese Witherspoon in *A Wrinkle in Time*.

Similar to artists like Kaling, entrepreneurs are non-conformists. Adam Grant, author and Wharton professor, explains the importance of thinking independently and creatively in his book *Originals*. According to Grant, "Originals are people who take the initiative to make their visions a reality. The hallmark of originality is rejecting the default and exploring whether a better option exists."[40]

Kaling's journey to stardom as an artist required the rejection of Hollywood's default view of conventional attractive performers.

While in college, Kaling decided to pursue her love for screenwriting. Her first notable creation was an off-Broadway comedy play about how Ben Affleck and Matt Damon wrote *Good Will Hunting*. She played Ben Affleck, and her friend played

40 Adam Grant, *Originals: How Non-Conformists Move the World* (New York: the Penguin Books, 2017), 1-352.

Matt Damon. Even after painstakingly working on the show, though, she didn't get offered to star in her own production as an actress. While the producers loved her writing, they told Kaling she wasn't attractive enough to star. Kaling was devastated, but the experience did teach her a lot about the field she was passionate about.[41]

In an interview with *Sunday Morning*, Kaling shared, "It showed me, for the first time, the harsh realities of Hollywood; they didn't think that we were television-friendly enough."[42]

That's when Kaling took acting and comedy into her own hands. Like Kaling's character Molly Patel in her movie *Late Night!*, she started performing her comedy in bars and landed a job working as a writer on *The Office*. While Kaling served as a writer, she was also able to add herself in as an actress, playing the side character Kelly Kapoor. Since there weren't existing roles for her in Hollywood, she had to write them herself. That's when Kaling first started using some of her own life to inspire her comedic writing.[43]

While Kaling loved creating *The Office*, she always knew she wanted to pursue her own creation and write a story that hadn't been featured on screen. From there, she created my all-time favorite show, *The Mindy Project*. She says she's always recognized for her confidence, but Kaling didn't feel that way at all when she started. However, what did occur to her was that no

41 CBS *Sunday Morning*, "Sunday Profile: Mindy Kaling," June 2, 2019, video, 7:21.

42 Ibid.

43 *The Off Camera Show*, "Mindy Kaling shares her early experiences in 'The Office' writers room," October 5, 2016, video, 2:56.

one who looked like her starred in what she watched. It was transformative for her to represent a group of people who had been left out of shows and express romantic love on television.[44]

She explains, "It's daunting. It's frightening. Because there's not many or any Indian female, comedy leads in anything. And that's when I get really jealous of the Danny McBrides and the Steve Carells."[45]

Comedians like McBride and Carell didn't have to think about what their portrayal of their character meant for white men. She was worried that she would create an Indian American character that made people question the identity. She felt she was responsible for writing a realistic and authentic story, but was cautious about writing one that made people believe it was a representation of all Indian American women.[46]

Inspiration for *The Mindy Project* came from her own experiences as an Indian American woman. Her ability to tell her story has opened the doors for other women to jump into the spotlight. Often, she finds herself in the company of those who thank her for her work. She didn't start her role with the aspiration to become that role model, though; instead, she wanted to write a story that represented her and her family, which shed light on overlooked races and genders in media.[47]

---

44 *The Paley Center for Media*, "The Mindy Project - Mindy Kaling On The Show's Origins And Development," July 24, 2014, video, 6:00.

45 Ibid.

46 Priya Arora, "Mindy Kaling's Netflix Show Tells a New Kind of Story: One Like Hers," *The New York Times*, April 27, 2020.

47 Brent Lang, "Mindy Kaling Created Her Own Opportunities (and Doesn't Plan on Stopping)," *Variety*, January 23, 2019.

Like Mindy, we need to be disruptive creators. If you find that you're not in the picture, put yourself into the story. Experiences and roles don't get handed out, so it's your job to create them.

Creative people embrace uncertainty and the unknown. While the path leads to hurdles and difficulty, it will also lead to more significant insights, experience, and knowledge.

Being a disruptive creator is easier said than done, though. We all fall into this space of comfort and let go of risk-taking. In fact, according to Valerie F. Reyna, Human Development professor at Cornell University, we lose our will for risk-taking. "Adolescents think very much about the odds," she says. "They think in a more precise way than adults do. Essentially, they are willing to take a calculated risk, whereas adults are much more likely to reject that risk even when the odds are in their favor."[48]

The idea of being comfortable is appealing to many people. You'll notice many people remain in jobs or relationships they're not happy with so they don't have to endure change. Naturally, people are intimidated by unfamiliarity and risk-taking. As popular business podcaster Tim Ferriss explains, people these days would rather be unhappy than uncertain.[49]

In fact, neuroscience research explains that "uncertainty registers in the brain much like an error does. It needs to

---

48 Jackie Swift, "How We Make Decisions and Take Risks," *Cornell Research,* November 7, 2019.

49 Scott Mautz, "Science Says This Is Why You Fear Change (and What to Do About it.)," *INC,* November 16, 2017.

be corrected before we can feel comfortable again, so we'd rather not have that hanging out there if we can avoid it."[50]

The art of being a disruptive creator can be daunting. But there are ways to ease the discomfort. *INC.* reviews the 4C's of change to consider:[51]

- **Career.** Calculated risk-taking is essential to continued growth in a career. "Research indicates that a fear of change is one of the single most career-limiting moves you can make."

- **Competence.** You have to believe that you are competent. You have the competence for change. "Research shows among all those who suffer from a fear of change that about half fear they won't be able to handle or thrive on the other side of a given change while the other half fear the process of or being prepared for change itself (and how painful it will be)."

- **Case.** You need to understand the case for change. If you know why a change is happening, you're less likely to view it as we view errors.

- **Core.** Change can make us feel untethered, like rock climbing without a harness. Instead, anchor yourself to what's important to you. There are things in life that won't change, like your values and connection with family and friends.

---

50 Ibid.

51 Ibid.

Change is inevitable, so why not explore being a disruptive creator?

Entrepreneur Dylan Field has utilized the 4Cs first-hand. The CEO of Figma, like Kaling, is a disruptive creator. During his sophomore year, he decided to drop out of Brown University to found his first company. Unlike most dropout CEOs though, Field was given $100,000 to drop out and pursue his passion and idea.[52] While in school, Field applied for the Thiel Fellowship, a program that pays students to leave their institutions and create things the world needs. The program believes dropping out of college provides a different perspective, and the most ambitious students can achieve through a more unique path if they're given the right resources.[53]

Even with a big idea in mind to create Figma, a vector graphics editor and primarily web-based prototyping tool, it took a long time to become a reality.[54] While the company was founded in 2012, it took them three years to actually start sending their software to beta users. Then, two years later, in 2017, they were finally able to offer a plan subscription model.

The years building Figma were full of uncertainty and Field had a lot to learn.

---

52   Rosalie Chen, "Here's how the CEO of Figma went from a computer science intern to the head of a $2 billion company that's challenging Adobe for the love of designers across Silicon Valley," *Business Insider*, October 1, 2020.

53   Ibid.

54   Ibid.

Having taken the road less traveled, and only having served as an intern before taking on the role of CEO, Field needed to find a way to manage a team and build the product he wanted. "I didn't know how to manage effectively. I didn't know the basics around how to have good judgment around who to hire. When we were ten people, I was a year into management. Usually, if you are a new manager, you manage a few people. I was trying to do this at the same time and get the product to market," Field said to *Business Insider*.[55]

In an interview on education, Field discussed the importance of exploring your passions and suggested students take extra time outside of school to delve deeper into them.[56] While I'm not saying you should drop out of college, though I've thought about it personally, I think it's essential to look at this as evidence that many successful creative people often take an unconventional route. Even if they don't know what they're doing, they take the risk. Field wasn't afraid to take a different path to pursue his ideas and interests, which led him to eye-opening experiences and innovations.

Instead of rejecting options right away, we should take the time to feel them out. Disruptive creators like Kaling and Field know that embracing uncertainty and discomfort is key to carving your own path. Or, as Mindy jokes, you could play things by ear.[57]

---

55 Ibid.

56 *Figma*, "Back to School? Marc Andreessen says get clear-eyed on what your education will give you," August 12, 2020, video, 58:37.

57 Brent Lang, "Mindy Kaling Created Her Own Opportunities (and Doesn't Plan on Stopping)," *Boston Herald*, January 23, 2019.

Reflecting on her commencement speech to her alma mater, Kaling joked, "I'd probably have listened to that [commencement] speech and thought, 'Whatever, you old bag. I'll be married to some hot rich guy and have a great career. I'll have it all.'"[58]

It's much easier said than done to become a disruptive creator. But don't think too long and hard about it. With the 4Cs in hand, there are so many options out there.

So, get in, we're going to create!

---

58 Ibid.

5.

MANIPULATE YOUR MOTIVATION

"Motivation reflects something unique about each one of us and allows us to gain valued outcomes like improved performance, enhanced well-being, personal growth, or a sense of purpose. Motivation is a pathway to change our way of thinking, feeling, and behaving."

- POSITIVE PSYCHOLOGY[59]

HARNESSING YOUR PASSION

Passion derives from *pati*, a Latin root that means *suffering*.[60] Passion spurs a pain that sufferers must work to suppress; meaning, it's the pain one is willing to endure to satisfy their drive. So why is passion important?

---

59   Beata Souders, "The Vital Importance and Benefits of Motivation," *Positive Psychology*, November 12, 2020.

60   Oxford Languages, Version 12.4., s.v. "Passion," Oxford University Press, 2021.

Why is passion relevant to creativity? We hear it all the time: *Find something you're passionate about.* Or *pursue your passion.* Passion is key because it helps you summon the strength needed to get through difficult times and tough decisions. In other words, passion is your fuel, especially during creative problem solving.

What passionate people do that helps lead to more creativity and advancement is celebrate every win and loss, no matter the size. Every time you celebrate your successes and failures, you recharge yourself, which helps when it feels like you're running on low steam. Take it from producer, director, and actor Jon Favreau.

Chef continues to be Favreau's most personal story. While it's not based on a true story, it still remains personal to him because of the way he created it. At first glance, the film seems to be out of Favreau's realm, especially as he has worked on blockbuster films and TV shows from *Elf* and *Iron Man* to *The Mandalorian*. While he's directed many amazing films, *Chef* still stands out as one of the most memorable and it's not just because the food looks so tasty!

What Favreau mastered was the ability to make a connection with the audience. You feel for his character, celebrity chef Carl Casper. You feel his downfalls and triumphs and you want him to succeed. To help add further authenticity to the story and character, Favreau drew from his own life for inspiration. As a child from a divorced household, he depicts Casper as a divorcé trying to mend his relationship with his son while pursuing his own dreams. He shares his own past emotions and attitudes through Carl's son Percy.

While preparing to star in his film, Favreau fell in love with the art of cooking. He studied under celebrity chef Roy Choi, who also inspired the concept for the film. In the movie, Favreau's character, Carl, faces a major setback in his career. While he had made it big as a well-known celebrity chef in California, he was living an incomplete and unfulfilling life. It's almost as if Favreau has drawn parallels between his own life as a filmmaker and Carl's life as a chef. Through his work on the film, he noted how he wanted to get back down to the roots of filmmaking. He wanted to create a story that resonated with people and took a step back from the major works he had built his career on.[61]

Chef gave Favreau the opportunity to find his original passion for entertainment. The film served as a way for him to refuel.

While working on *Chef*, Favreau was so inspired by his newly rekindled passion for entertainment that he wanted to continue the story further; he decided to combine his new love for cooking with his passion for directing. He called up Choi, and they started a Netflix show called *The Chef Show*.[62] I was able to sit down with Choi and he spoke about his view on the pathway to creativity.

Before meeting Favreau, Choi dropped out of law school to pursue his passion for cooking and opened his first food truck. He knew it was the right move for him when he

---

61 Cory Stillman, "Chef Movie True Story: How Much Is Based On Jon Favreau's Real Life," *ScreenRant*, December 3, 2020.

62 *The Hollywood Reporter*, "Jon Favreau & Roy Choi on Chef Inspiration: Rule Breakers," June 7, 2019, Video, 4:11.

found himself putting everything he had into his work. He knew law school wasn't the right path when he felt something was missing. Differing from his work in law school, Choi felt a great deal of pride as a chef. He told me, "When Kogi first started twelve years ago, and when I realized that something very special was happening, I was in a creative mind of where I had to be a bit of a portal and a conduit to what was really happening on the streets. And to be almost a bit of a microphone to the immediacy and the visceral life that exists, that it was kind of a voice of the voiceless type of thing."

For him the most important stories are the authentic ones, and he aims to tell those stories through work as a celebrity chef and author: "In a way, I'm documenting and trying to bring to life the people and places that raised me, that I feel are part of who I am, that I'm representing. I found a place in this creative world, and a voice by telling and expressing the stories that I grew up around."

One of his favorite projects was *The Chef Show*, which features himself cooking with Favreau and a guest celebrity. On the show, Choi and Favreau just have fun and cook in the kitchen. "That is a product of two like-minded souls, Jon and myself, being people that believe in the pathway to creativity," he says. "The end result, itself, was us not taking ourselves too seriously and still having a very DIY development, with imperfections in cooking and creating."

And the show is just that. If you watch *The Chef Show*, you'll find two friends who are just having fun in the kitchen. You can feel their excitement for what they do and it's infectious.

Something Choi noted about the success of the show was that they never lost themselves as creators: "Even though [Jon and I] have gotten a bit older and achieved certain things, we have never lost that part of ourselves, as far as creativity goes. So, the show itself was based on the premise of 'Let's turn the camera on, and let's just cook and figure it out.' From there, there was never a script or any grand purpose to proving how much we can cook. That was just a real moment. I guess that's what comes from having independence in art."

According to Choi, the best moments in his life are those that required risk-taking. When he decided to drop out of law school, he took one of his biggest life risks. He strayed from his parents' path and came to understand his own passion for cooking. Similarly, for Favreau, the greatest lesson he's learned is how important it is to take risks when you're passionate about something. He notes that his best work came about because he believed in what he was creating. Like in *Chef*, Favreau's ability to get back to the roots of filmmaking made his final product even more impactful and memorable. Favreau believes his best work is a result of his passion.[63]

Like Favreau and Choi, we need to reflect and rediscover what excites us. Looking back, why did you start doing something? What drew you to it in the first place? Where are you now? Once you understand your journey, you'll understand more about the root of your passion. And once you rediscover your passion, you'll have the fuel you need to keep going.

---

63 *The Hollywood Reporter*, "Jon Favreau & Roy Choi on Chef Inspiration: Rule Breakers," June 7, 2019, video, 4:11.

DEFINING YOUR PURPOSE

Passion alone isn't enough, though. While it serves as great fuel, we require a vehicle to take us where we want to go. That's where purpose comes in. Unlocking your passion and purpose are key to tapping into your creative ability.

Defining your purpose can sound overwhelming. I'm not saying you need to know your life's meaning or uncover why you're here on the planet, but it's important to know why you function the way that you do. What motivates you? To manipulate your motivation, you need to define your purpose.

One day, my little sister came barging into my room and announced that she was going to run for student council. It was her first week of high school, and she couldn't wait to get involved in all the activities the school had to offer. She reminded me of myself in high school—so ready to take on everything at once, signing up for every club possible.

She was so excited. In fact, her friends had already helped her develop phrases to advertise her campaign around the school. "How do you like 'Cheerio for Lirio?' How about 'I'm serio. Vote Lirio?' Or my friends said I should try 'Don't Be Delirio, Vote Lirio.'" She continued scrolling through her messages with ideas. She then went on to talk about how she had already collected her twenty-five signatures and met with her dean to get approval to make it on the ballot. All she needed was her personal statement.

"What should I write?" she asked me, frantically. My sister is some-one who always likes to get things done significantly *ahead* of time. I recall laughing as I went over to her desk because I knew she had more than a week to submit everything, and she was already stressing over missing one last piece. I looked down at her computer as she sat at her desk. The form read:

DON'T FORGET:

Your candidate statement is due at the same time as these nomination papers. Everything must be submitted on Schoology by TUESDAY.

There was no straightforward question or prompt; they wanted to hear from the candidate about anything they were willing to share about their campaign. My first question for her was, "Why are you running?"

There was a slight pause. "I don't know," she shrugged. "What do you think I should write about?"

"What do you mean? Why are you so excited to run?" I couldn't stop thinking about her long list of catchphrases and sayings; she was so excited and prepared to run, but she had no idea why. "What got you to collect twenty-five signatures? Why are you drawn to do this?"

"I don't know. I think it'll be fun?"

"Yes, but what else?" I laughed. "You have to figure out why you're running. I can only help you with the writing once you know why."

Understanding your motivation and purpose is not only key to succeeding in any creative endeavor, but crucial for society to function at its best. When you decide a certain course of action, you need to be able to tie that decision to a reason.

A successful community depends on people being able to achieve at their full potential, according to Harvard University's Center on the Developing Child. Their research states, "A complex set of intertwined social and biological factors influences people's motivation to participate actively and productively in schools, jobs, and communities...and to persevere in the face of setbacks."[64]

By breaking down our own motivation, we're able to manipulate our performance, growth and wellbeing.

For most people, there are only a few motivators:[65]

1. Money

2. Autonomy

3. Recognition

4. Culture of Respect, Trust, and Rapport

5. Engagement in the Work Itself

And there are two main forms of motivation:

---

64 National Scientific Council on the Developing Child, "Understanding Motivation: Building the Brain Architecture That Supports Learning, Health, and Community Participation," *Center on the Developing Child*, January 20, 2021.

65 Ibid.

Extrinsic motivation is reward-based. When you are extrinsically motivated, you do something to gain some form of external reward. According to professors Edward Deci and Richard Ryan, the **Self-Determination Theory** (SDT) explains how rewards and praise affect motivation; they often provide positive effects on an event. There are hidden costs to certain types of rewards, though. Certain rewards "can undermine intrinsic motivation by decreasing the sense of autonomy and competence."[66]

Intrinsic motivation comes from within. When you're intrinsically motivated, you engage in something because you enjoy it and get personal satisfaction. Understanding what motivates you and finding intrinsically motivating things makes all the difference in what you do. When you come across a project that excites you, make sure you're excited about it for the right reasons.

When one is intrinsically motivated, they perform better and can be more creative. While extrinsic motivation can produce almost immediate effects, especially for kids, it isn't as effective for creativity or learning. Intrinsic motivation creates people with real interest and passion for what they are doing. They want to continue exploring it and building upon it, and this holds true for any workplace.[67] McKinsey data shows that "employees who are intrinsically motivated are 32 percent more committed to their job, have 46 percent higher job satisfaction, and perform 16 percent better than other employees."[68]

---

66   "Theory," Self Determination Theory, accessed February 28, 2021.

67   Beata Souders, "The Vital Importance and Benefits of Motivation," *Positive Psychology*, November 12, 2020.

68   Michael Bazigos and Emily Caruso, "Why Frontline Workers are Disengaged," *McKinsey & Company*, March 2, 2016.

Take the founder and CEO of Happily, Sarah Shewey, for example. Happily is a global events company; they specifically work to create carbon-zero events. Shewey, an environmentalist, has spoken about the importance of sustainability.

She created Happily with the intent of addressing the climate crisis. While working at TED Conferences, she noticed how much waste and environmental harm events had on the world. Today, they lead with the following values:[69]

1. Reduce waste

2. Represent diverse voices

3. Reinvest in local and forgotten communities

With those goals in mind, she has successfully grown to support fifty thousand independent event specialists since 2012.[70] While extrinsic motivation is effective, it's not nearly as effective as intrinsic motivation. So, next time you partake in something, consider why you're doing it and what the outcomes will be.

Understanding what motivates you and finding things that are intrinsically motivating make all the difference in what you do. When you come across a project that excites you, ask yourself why it excites you and what your motivation is. For my sister, she was excited about running for student council because she wanted to serve as a representative for her fellow

---

69 "About," Happily, accessed March 11, 2021.

70 Ibid.

students in planning events for them to bond and grow. She ended up writing this as her personal statement:

"Hello, my name is Adrienne Lirio! If I get elected, my main objective is not simply to make our freshman year amazing and fun but to also help make our class a family. I know more than ever that we need unity. Freshman year is a big transition, especially with us now doing online school! It's not only a big adjustment academically but socially. It makes it exceptionally hard to make any new friends at all. The closest thing to human interaction with other students is when we go into those awkward breakout rooms. I know, for sure, no one enjoys that! All jokes aside, I want to solve the issues by having monthly freshman competitions, game nights, and movie nights. (Marvel marathons, anyone?) I think we should actually get to know each other. Not just with names and faces, but with genuine friendships. We should all aspire to create a supportive environment for everyone. I want you all to know that I'm here to listen, help, and just to be there for anyone that needs a friend. The coronavirus has taken many things away from us. However, I hope that it won't take our sense of connection with each other."

Once you understand what excites you and what drives you, you'll have the ability to uncover and manipulate your own motivation.

6.

THE POWER OF PERSEVERANCE

———

UNCLE IROH'S ADVICE: LIFE IS LIKE A TUNNEL

Thomas Edison once said, "Genius is 1 percent inspiration and 99 percent perspiration," and that was definitely the case for the team behind the beloved animated TV show *Avatar: The Last Airbender*.[71] The creators, Bryan Konietzko and Michael Dante DiMartino actualize how persistence and pride in one's work are crucial to any creative endeavor's success.

Konietzko and DiMartino met when they were in college at the Rhode Island School of Design (RISD). Throughout college, they had both shared the same dream to create a TV show. Equipped with their artistic abilities following college, they went on to pitch shows individually. Unsuccessful, they worked in the animation industry for years and still hoped for their big break.[72]

---

71 Dictionary.com, (Oxford: Lexico, 2008), s.v. "Genius is one percent inspiration and ninety-nine percent perspiration."

72 *UltimateKorraTV*, "Avatar: The Last Airbender Documentary (Full)-Avatar Spirits," May 18, 2013, video, 32:19.

After years apart, they decided to work together officially. Having background and experience in animation, they went to speak with Nickelodeon to ask what the studio was looking for in the next show. Konietzko and DiMartino shared about how they wanted to create a TV show centered around legend and lore.[73] The animation head at the studio said, "Sounds great, but make sure you put it into a kid's point of view."[74] Konietzko and DiMartino weren't quite sure where they were headed, but they knew this was a significant first step.[75]

They labored over new ideas and had only two weeks to prepare their pitch. If you hear the way they came up with the idea, it's pretty funny. You might look at their initial drawings and think, *How did they get from here to there?* It all started because Konietzko drew two robots: a polar bear and a monkey with an arrow on his head. They weren't entirely sold on creating a show on robots, though. Concurrently, DiMartino had found a new love for arctic exploration; he had been watching documentaries on it for hours during his free time. He suggested the idea to Konietzko: What if they had something happen in the South Pole? On another day, after yoga, Konietzko had a new concept to draw a bald kid, inspired by DiMartino's bald head. He put the robot monkey's arrow on the character's head, and from there, they created Aang, the protagonist in the show. They then combined this with DiMartino's new interest in the South Pole. They described it as, "There's an air guy along with these water people trapped in a snowy wasteland... and maybe some fire people are

73 Ibid.
74 Ibid.
75 Ibid.

pressing down on them." That's what sparked the creation of the four nations—Water, Earth, Fire, and Air. They were so excited about the concept that they created Aang's world in a couple of days.[76]

They went back to Nickelodeon faster than anyone thought they would and recalled pitching the concept to the animation head for far longer than expected. They had drawings and sketches on the world, characters, ideas, and plot. The head of animation stopped them mid-presentation. Konietzko and DiMartino were in shock; they thought they had messed up the pitch. To their relief, he told them the show was unique.[77] After years of work in the animation business, Konietzko and DiMartino finally got their big break to work on their own creation.

With Avatar in development, they had time to create the show they had always dreamed of making. While the show and its creation appear glamorous, the creators agreed it was nothing like that.[78] Producing an animated television program is an arduous process. It involves dozens of people working long hours to create every single frame. On average, there are twenty-four frames per second, which means there are around 33,000 pictures in a thirty-minute program when you include the seven minutes of commercial break.[79] They

76 *UltimateKorraTV*, "Avatar: The Last Airbender Documentary (Full)-Avatar Spirits," May 18, 2013, Video, 32:19.

77 Ibid.

78 Ibid.

79 Brandon Baker, "Infrequently Asked Questions: How does 2-D animation work?," *PhillyVoice*, April 5, 2017.

did a lot of tedious labor to bring the show together and the work was engulfing; they'd find themselves working six to seven days, fifteen-hour days per week.[80]

Going to conventions always energized them, though. Every time they walked into a room with fans wearing the characters' costumes, their faces lit up with excitement. Despite the long hours and heavy workload, they found the motivation in their fans' support and love of the show to push through.[81]

As they signed posters, fan after fan came up to thank them profusely for creating a world in which they could connect and escape. The two said that made their work meaningful.[82] Before attending conventions, they saw themselves as artists who created in the background and would hide away and draw in their office. They didn't know how many people they would connect with through their show.[83] Their persistence to keep delivering a great story and show for the people who loved it made it what it is today.

Konietzko and DiMartino embody what it means to be persistent and prideful in one's work.

Like the creation of a startup, persistence is crucial in creating an animated TV show. A study from Harvard Business Review noted that we often undervalue the benefits of persistence. In a

---

80 *UltimateKorraTV*, "Avatar: The Last Airbender Documentary (Full)- Avatar Spirits," May 18, 2013, Video, 32:19.

81 Ibid.

82 Ibid.

83 Ibid.

series of experiments, Behavioral Science Professor Brian Lucas and Professor of Management Loran Nordgren observed how people often underestimated the "number of ideas they could generate while solving a creative challenge."[84]

In one experiment, they brought in twenty-four university students before Thanksgiving break. They asked them to spend ten minutes coming up with as many ideas of dishes to serve at Thanksgiving dinner as possible. Then, they asked them to predict how many more ideas they would generate if they persisted for another ten minutes. On average, the students predicted that they would generate around ten new ideas. They had them continue to come up with ideas for another ten minutes. And Lucas and Nordgren found that the students were actually able to generate around fifteen new ideas.[85]

They conducted several other studies and had the same results. They asked professional comedians to generate punch lines and adults to come up with advertisement slogans. In every experiment, they found that the participants underestimated their ability to generate new ideas if they persisted. Lastly, they conducted a study on the creativity of the participants' ideas. They collected the ideas and asked a separate group to rate the creativity of them. They found that the ideas generated while persisting were rated more creative than ideas generated in the first round.[86]

---

84 Loran Nordgren and Brian Lucas, "Your Best Ideas Are Often Your Last Ideas" *HBR*, January 26, 2021.

85 Ibid.

86 Ibid.

But persistence isn't the only thing that leads to creative success. According to psychologist and author Angela Duckworth, passion is just as important as persistence: "I think the misunderstanding—or, at least, one of them—is that it's only the perseverance part that matters [...] But I think that the passion piece is at least as important. I mean, if you are really, really tenacious and dogged about a goal that's not meaningful to you and not interesting to you—then that's just drudgery. It's not just determination—it's having a direction that you care about."[87]

Like Konietzko and DiMartino, possessing pride in your work is crucial in any creative endeavor. In a study, David DeSteno, professor of psychology at Northeastern University, found that people "who were induced to feel proud of their work devoted more time and effort to solving challenging problems."[88] Persistence and pride are directly linked. Pride in one's work leads to more endurance to perform.

So, just believe in your ambition and follow through. ***Don't edit your ambition.*** As people say, the ability to execute separates the dreamers from the doers. Konietzko and DiMartino knew what they wanted to do once they completed college and pursued it despite the challenges. While their original pitches were rejected time and time again, they didn't allow their failures to set them back.

---

87 Melissa Dahl, "Don't Believe the Hype About Grit, Pleads the Scientist Behind the Concept," *The Cut*, May 9, 2016.

88 David DeSteno, "The Connection Between Pride and Persistence," *HBR*, August 22, 2016.

Konietzko highlighted the importance of just going into the field you're interested in and finding a path to what you want. He started in character development for animations, pitched his idea, and found a path to creating his own TV show. They used their imagination to develop Aang and built one of the most loved animated TV shows today. And after nineteen years of reaching people with their content, in 2021, Konietzko and DiMartino announced that they'll serve as Chief Creative Officers at the newly formed Avatar Studios backed by Nickelodeon and Paramount+.[89]

As Derek Andersen, CEO and founder of Startup Grind, the world's largest community for startups, entrepreneurs, and creators, said at a conference I helped organize, "When you pitch an investor and they say no, don't take it personally. Get up and go on to the next one and just tell a better story." An investor's "no" just means they don't believe yet, so it's your job to continue persisting.

Like any startup founder, Konietzko and DiMartino needed to find a way to articulate their creative vision. Skilled animators and storytellers need to be strong in artistic talent, generating ideas, and collaboration with others. Like your traditional startup, Konietzko and DiMartino got a backer to support their ambition. Their key to success was their endurance to follow through when the work was difficult; persistence is crucial for any successful creator and entrepreneur. The ability to push forward and through to the finish line when things get tough differentiates successful creators from the rest.

---

89   Rick Porter, "'Avatar: Last Airbender' Expanded Universe Set at Nickelodeon," *The Hollywood Reporter*, February 24, 2021.

Take it from Uncle Iroh in Season Two's episode "The Cross-roads of Destiny": "Sometimes life is like this tunnel. You can't always see the light at the end of the tunnel, but if you keep moving, you will come to a better place."[90]

---

90 *Avatar: The Last Airbender,* "The Guru/The Crossroads of Destiny," Netflix video, 47:00, December 1, 2006.

7.

EMBRACING AUTHENTICITY

———

Authenticity is scary.

There's no doubt about that.

But it's fundamental to creative success.

Being authentic only elevates your creative endeavors, as it builds your identity, gives substance to what you're offering, and enables people to relate and engage with you. Not to mention, honesty in one's work makes every day more meaningful and enjoyable. Simply put, "Being authentic means staying true to who you are, what you do, and who you serve."[91]

As author Neil Pasricha summarized in a TED Talk, "When you're authentic, you end up following your heart, and you

———

91 James Noble, "Truth Will Out — Why Authenticity is the Key to Growing Your Business," *Neil Patel*, January 24, 2020.

put yourself in places and situations and in conversations that you love and that you enjoy. You meet people that you like talking to, you go places you've dreamt about, and you end up following your heart and feeling very fulfilled."[92]

Singer-songwriter Billie Eilish and Finneas O'Connell are artists who employ this power well.

CREATE FROM THE COMFORT OF YOUR BEDROOM

Billie's Carpool Karaoke with James Corden is one of my favorite videos of her, and that isn't just because she's a phenomenal vocalist. I've watched it on repeat because I'm in awe of her authenticity. In the clip, she walks James through the bedroom where she and her brother Finneas wrote and produced their Grammy-winning album *When We Fall Asleep, Where Do We Go?* She walks into her house, a two-bedroom in California, and waves her hand up toward a whiteboard on the wall. She points at each scribble of text and explains that she and Finneas drew bullet points with every song name on their album with a black expo marker. The room isn't anything fancy, the bed is full of rainbow flower pillows, and there's a computer set up with all of Finneas' production tools.[93] In an interview, Finneas recalled creating and recording the entire album in his bedroom. He pointed at his bed, "She'd sit here, and I'd just bring the microphone over to where she is."[94] According to Finneas, his sister recorded

---

92 Neil Pasricha, "The 3 A's of Awesome," Lecture, TED, 2010.

93 *The Late Late Show With James Corden*, "Billie Eilish Carpool Karaoke," December 20, 2019, Video, 17:04.

94 *AWAL*, "SPACES: Inside the Tiny Bedroom Where FINNEAS and Billie Eilish Are Redefining Pop Music," April 2, 2019, Video, 5:00.

pretty much every vocal for the album sitting on his bed with her legs crossed. "That's kind of insane," he recalled.[95]

While recording at home, Billie and Finneas had an opportunity to create something deeply personal and unique. They played around with sounds in the house—from recording the flicker of lighting matches in the bathroom to the infamous recording of Billie taking out her Invisalign. According to Finneas, working in their childhood home made their work more intimate.[96]

"There's a kind of private feeling to what we're doing because we're not at a recording studio where different people are every day," he said. "This is our house, and it's where we live, and it's where we have experienced everything that allows us to make some kind of music that feels wholeheartedly exposed as far as who we really are as people and as siblings."[97]

Billie and Finneas found their musical genius and success through their desire to be open, honest, and vulnerable. And for Finneas, there's power in creating your own sound: "I just think when you build your own sound, it's a very fast way to make your music feel very unique."[98]

A strength they both have is staying true to their respective voices; they know whether a song speaks to them and expresses their own identity. While they both have a hand in writing each

---

95 Ibid.

96 *AWAL*, "SPACES: Inside the Tiny Bedroom Where FINNEAS and Billie Eilish Are Redefining Pop Music," April 2, 2019, Video, 5:00.

97 Ibid.

98 Ibid.

other's music and often are sitting in a room together coming up with a rhyme or tune, they understand what their artistic voices are and want to stay true to them. They decide to release music under Billie's name when they know that the track is something that Billie feels and wants to express and share with the world.[99]

Finneas has employed this skill with others while working with various artists like Selena Gomez, Demi Lovato, Halsey, and Justin Bieber.

He muses, "If I'm writing a song with Billie, I'm just trying to help her tell whatever story she's trying to tell. Similarly, with other artists, if you're writing and you know that someone else's voice is going to be the voice telling the story, it should be a language that fits them. I think that's the biggest key. 'Are these words that she would say?' Everybody has a different vocabulary, a different way of putting sentences together, and the easiest way to tell if a song wasn't written by someone is if it doesn't fit their vernacular. So, I try to match whatever I'm helping them make to whoever they seem to be. A lot of that also, to be fair, is asking an artist how they feel about it. If you come up with a line, even if an artist really likes it and is like, 'That's a really cool line,' it's like 'Yeah, but can you wear it? Is it a thing you'd feel comfortable with singing every time?'"[100]

For example, Finneas wrote both "Ocean Eyes" and "When the Party's Over" and decided to give them to Billie to listen to and consider. She loved the vibe and felt like they expressed

---

99 *SiriusXM*, "How Does Finneas Decide if a Song is for Him or for Billie Eilish," October 28, 2019, Video, 4:52.

100 Ibid.

a part of her, and both siblings realized it would be best for the songs to be released and performed by her. For Finneas, telling an authentic and powerful story through music is far more important than releasing a song under his own name. An amazing team, they understand what's best for each other's artistic expression. For them, self-expression is the most important trait in their music. Some artists and producers focus on whether or not the track sounds good, but for Billie and Finneas, they focus first on whether or not the song is honest. "Do I really feel this?" Finneas asks. "Can I really perform this every show and mean every word of it, and also, is it so honest that I'm a little worried about it?"[101]

But the process isn't always easy. As the newest award-winning artists, Billie and Finneas feel constant pressure to produce hits at the expense of their authenticity. In Billie's most recent documentary, *The World's a Little Blurry*, the two argue about making tracks for the album. While creating her debut album, the record company kept insisting on producing a new hit. While in Finneas' room one day, they found themselves between a rock and a hard place. While Billie loves performing, she loves what she does even more if she connects with the music. Whenever creating music, Billie is always determined to remain authentic above all else; she refuses to sacrifice her own artistry to produce a conventional hit song.[102]

Despite her vulnerability and honesty, though, she's faced a lot of scrutiny when it comes to her music.

---

101 *SiriusXM*, "How Does Finneas Decide if a Song is for Him or for Billie Eilish," October 28, 2019, Video, 4:52.

102 R.J Cutler, director, 2021, *Billie Eilish: The World's A Little Blurry*, Production Neon Apple TV+.

"People are always like 'It's so dark, like, write happy music,'" Billie shared. "But I'm never feeling happy, so why would I write about things I don't know about? I feel the dark things. I feel them very strongly. Why would I not talk about them?"[103]

When asked about how she decided to cover important topics like depression and anxiety—both very personal subjects—Billie said, "I never decided to. I was never like, 'I'm going to talk about this, and I'm going to talk about this.' I just talked about what I was feeling and talked about why it was bad or why it was good or why it was whatever, and then it became this 'Oh, she's making a statement.' Which I actually love because I didn't realize I was, and now that I think about it, I realized how many people aren't talking about that kind of stuff."[104]

Being authentic and honest is scary, Finneas explains. But it's worth it.

"Any time I get really scared of a thing I'm like, 'You know what? This is probably what I should be putting out.'"[105]

"I look into the crowd, and I see all these faces. So many different feelings and heartbreak," Billie describes. "Every single person in there is going through something good or bad or

---

103 Ibid.

104 Ibid.

105 Nicole Almeida, "Wholehearted Obsession: A Conversation With Finneas," *Atwood Magazines*, April 27, 2018.

horrible or amazing. And the least I can do is make art that I make because I have the same problems."[106]

There's real power in authenticity. While it can be scary, it opens up opportunities that weren't always evident. Authenticity is vulnerable, but it allows us to create from the heart and connect with people who relate.

You can create from anywhere and out of anything. Embrace the power of authenticity and get started from the comfort of your own bedroom. Focus on creating honest work. What worked for Billie and Finneas especially was their authenticity and ability to expose their true selves, exploring their love for music without the world's distractions and standards. Don't focus on the noise around you; take that noise and make it your own track.

* * *

BEING VULNERABLE IS GOOD

With all that said, though, it's hard to be authentic. The idea of expressing oneself fully is daunting. We fear authenticity because it requires three things:

- **Vulnerability.** When you choose courage over comfort.

- **Transparency.** When you practice your values rather than stating them.

---

106 R.J. Cutler, director, 2021, *Billie Eilish: The World's A Little Blurry*, Production Neon Apple TV+.

- **Integrity**. When you do what's right over what isn't.

According to therapist and author Darlene Lancer, we're scared of authenticity primarily due to our fear of rejection.[107] Instead of focusing on our unease toward authenticity, though, we need to center ourselves on the positives.

Understanding yourself and expressing yourself is crucial in any creative endeavor because it allows you to find problems and better connect with others in the same space.

Here are things you should consider:

YOU WON'T CONNECT WITH EVERYONE, BUT YOU'LL FIND *YOUR* PEOPLE.

Not everyone will support what you're interested in or excited about, but that just means you'll find the people who are. While working on this book, I came across a few doubters. While entertaining a guest with my family one evening, my parents explained how I was writing and publishing my first book. My parents were so excited to share the news with anyone they could, but instead of hearing the usual quick, "That's great for you! Let me know when it comes out," the guest replied, "Oh, really. Ha-ha, well you'll both have to get used to her living at home and being a starving author."

I know they intended it to be a joke, but it felt like a punch in the gut. Why did they belittle my ambition and dream

---

107 Darlene Lancer, "The Power of Authenticity: 6 Steps to Achieve it," *Medium*, July 25, 2016.

of becoming an author? Why did they have assumptions without even getting to know me? These kinds of naysayers are common, and you'll bump into them all the time.

All you can do is embrace the idea that there will be people who support you and people who won't. Being authentic doesn't mean everyone will like you. It means you'll find an even better community of people, like my amazing author community, who will really connect with you, which is far more important than being accepted by everyone.

YOU'LL FEEL MORE FULFILLED WITH YOUR WORK.
In a study on authenticity, "researchers found that people who scored higher on a measure of authentic living reported greater happiness, more positive emotions, and higher self-esteem than people who reported being less authentic." In addition, people who felt authentic noted having better relationships and more personal growth.[108]

The happier and more confident you are, the more creative you can be. According to positivity author Bryan Hutchinson, "When you are happy, life seems so much more alive and beautiful, you become filled with inspiration and motivation."[109] And when you're inspired and motivated, you feel more fulfilled.

---

108 Alex Mathew Wood, P. Alex Linley, John Maltby and Michael Baliousi, "The Authentic Personality: A Theoretical and Empirical Conceptualization and the Development of the Authenticity Scale," *ResearchGate*, July 2008.

109 Bryan Hutchinson, "How Patagonia Keeps Its Brand Message Authentic In The Midst of An Activewear Boom," *PositiveWriter*, accessed March 18, 2021.

THERE'S A DIFFERENT ENERGY ABOUT PEOPLE WHO ARE GENUINELY EXCITED ABOUT WHAT THEY DO.

There's a certain spark in them; they know what they're talking about and have compelling reasons for pursuing it. I remember when someone highlighted a certain spark I had. I was interviewing for a startup role, and they ran through the classic questions: "What are you working on right now?" "What are you interested in?" "Why are you interested in working with us?"

For the first question, I started talking about my excitement toward writing and publishing this book. I explained my thoughts on the subject, the research and interviews I had conducted so far, and my overall love for writing. At that moment, I didn't realize how long I had been talking. The interviewer smiled at me, and I paused. "Wow, you really just lit up talking about that. I could see it in your face," I recall her saying. "That's something we're looking for on our team."

I got the job, and my manager noted it was because of my excitement and enthusiasm for what I did.

Authenticity is the opposite of shame. Being yourself allows you to reveal your own humanity. Think about it this way, when you hide who you are, you often sacrifice your needs and interests.

Creativity means questioning who you are, so don't be scared of it! Showing people who you are and what you love will only lead to more possibilities. Being vulnerable is key to forging strong relationships, and remember—nothing amazing comes easily.

DIFFERENTIATING YOUR BUSINESS

Aside from artists, brands have seen the power of authenticity work wonders, too; it differentiates your creation.

Take successful brands Patagonia and Dove for example, both exemplify the importance of authenticity in one's work. Good brands have a purpose: a reason for existing. But the purpose needs to be authentic and honest.

Patagonia's purpose is to "build the best product, cause no unnecessary harm, and use business to inspire and implement solutions to the environmental crisis."[110] They work toward this by basing every decision—designing products, recruiting staff, and working on ads—on these metrics. This authenticity makes customers feel like investing in a Patagonia jacket is worthwhile. The company doesn't cut corners and works toward a greater mission.

Dove took a similar approach. In 2017, they launched the Dove Real Beauty Pledge, which promises the following: "We always feature real women, never models. We portray women as they are in real life. We help girls build confidence and self-esteem." In a study, Dove found that seven in ten women didn't feel represented in the media and advertising. According to Sophie Van Ettinger, global Dove vice president it means that "they are rendered invisible, and that has a lasting impact on how girls and women participate in society."[111] Pinpointing their target market, Dove has seen great success in their campaigns.

---

110 "Core Values," Patagonia, accessed March 18, 2021.

111 Jennifer Fisher, "How Unilever's Dove Delivers on Its Brand Purpose," *The Wall Street Journal*, May 13, 2020.

For over ten years, Dove has educated over "twenty million people on body confidence and self-esteem and has become the biggest provider of self-esteem education of its kind."[112]

As retail consultant, Robert Burke explains, "It's not just enough for [the customer today] to run out and buy, say, a ruffle top. They want to know everything about it: what it stands for, who's behind it, how it was made, and the type of person it represents."[113]

It's clear that authenticity helps differentiate you and your work, and people take notice. I experienced this first-hand while working at a local cupcake store.

IDENTIFYING A NEED

I've always loved baking, from chocolate chip cookies and banana bread to fruit tarts and French macaroons. While in school, I found baking to be one of the most relaxing activities. In high school, I set my eyes on a local cupcakery. I *really* wanted to work there. We had been purchasing cakes there regularly ever since it opened, and I thought it would be an amazing experience. I wanted to see how two local Bostonians found a way to take what they loved and create a successful small business.

I went into the store for an interview one day right after school. Bakers were chatting in the background over the oven timer's

---

112 "The 'Dove Real Beauty Pledge,'" Dove, accessed March 18, 2021.

113 Maura Brannigan, "How Patagonia Keeps Its Brand Message Authentic In The Midst of An Activewear Boom," *Fashionista*, June 27, 2016.

sound going off, and I saw students rolling cake pops and helping customers get their much-deserved cupcakes. I could smell the freshly baked, sweet, red velvet buttery cake in the air and I was so excited because I could feel the passion and love everyone had for what they did. They had smiles on their faces as they baked and prepared treats for customers. They were proud to create something that made people happy and that was key to people's best memories.

While sitting across a table designed like a cupcake, I could see how much Adie, the head-baker and ringleader, loved her job. She was excited to hear about my interest in the store. As I shared my experience, she recalled how my mom was one of the first customers to order a treat. She remembered so many customers by name.

Through my time working at Treat Cupcake Bar, I learned more about the story behind the successful small business.

What's really amazing is both Adie Sprague and Dave Laliberte, who calls himself the "money guy," didn't think they would go into creating a cupcake store. After completing her undergraduate degree at Brandeis, Adie decided to continue her education by getting her master's in architecture. While she was going through this, Adie questioned whether or not pursuing architecture was the right thing for her. By chance, she bumped into a post saying that somebody was looking to hire a baker to help create a cupcake bakery in Needham, Massachusetts.

Before opening Treat, Dave had worked in the financial industry. When he retired, he decided to start his second career by creating a small business in his town. Dave wanted to find something that Needham didn't have and that they needed. For years, he watched kids come out of school and go to Walgreens or the grocery store. He noticed they didn't have a place to spend time. That's when the concept for Treat was born. He wanted to create a place where kids and adults alike could come in, sit down, and enjoy the best cupcake around.

The funny part was Dave didn't know much, or anything, about cupcakes, and that's where Adie came in.

Adie didn't have any culinary or professional baking experience, but she was excited and had ideas for making the business a success. That was enough to convince Dave. At twenty-four, Adie created the store by figuring out the recipes, designing the store layout, and learning about the staffing and resources needed.

So, that's how it all started. Adie came up with all of the recipes herself, creating and mastering all of the techniques in her small apartment in Brookline. She recalls that while all of her friends went out for work, she stayed in the kitchen all day baking up a storm. Adie created your classic chocolate and vanilla cakes, learned how to make a unique red velvet cake, and created the classic Oreo cake and the beloved carrot cakes. Once she had the base recipes down, she invited people over or went to events with her sweet treats. She was determined to get advice and thoughts on the desserts. While reflecting on the experience, she laughed when she explained how she used to set a piece of paper by each cupcake and asked people to name it. That's where she got some of the more silly names or figured out what was popular.

Something they remembered is having to find a way to make themselves unique. During the time, there were hundreds of cupcake stores in New England. They needed something that made them stick out. That's where the Make Your Own Cupcake option was born. In addition to Pick A Treat, they created a Make Your Own station so people could come in and pick their own frosting and toppings. A few years later, they also created an assortment of gluten, dairy, egg, soy, and nut-free options. They realized there was a demand for allergy-friendly cupcakes, and they were happy to oblige. These creative options have allowed for more people to find the bakery.

In the world of businesses and startups, the real driver in creativity and innovation is "experience and know-how," according to serial entrepreneur Patrick Hull. Take Mark Zuckerberg for example. Myspace had already been the "it" social networking site. Zuckerberg hadn't created the first social networking platform. His big breakthrough for Facebook was creating a space that met the right audience's needs.[114] A successful business identifies a need and meets it. That's the secret to success: finding ways to differentiate yourself.

After ten years of this experience, both Dave and Adie can't believe how far they've come. Looking back, Dave explains how he wanted to find a way to put his money in and invest into something that he knew would be meaningful. He wanted to find a way to create a place where people loved to work, and where people could relax and grab a cupcake.

---

114 Patrick Hull, "It's Not All About The Money," *New York Times*, March 11, 2014.

Adie and Dave's genuine interest in being a part of people's best memories and serving those in need of allergy-friendly desserts has led to Treat's ultimate success. Being true to your brand differentiates the best businesses from the rest.

Remember, if you are authentic and genuine in meeting people's needs, you'll find success in any creative endeavor that you pursue. While it can be daunting, it's worth the risk.

PART 3

ENTREPRENEURSHIP AS AN ART

8.

CREATING YOUR
OWN LUCK

———

AN EYE FOR OPPORTUNITY

Often, people have ideas that they think could become a business one day. How many times have you heard the phrase, "Wouldn't it be an amazing idea to _____?" Most of the time, it does seem like it would be a great idea. But, more often than not, we end up finding an issue in the concept. And you'd probably be right about the issue, because usually the "amazing idea" isn't all that good after all. A critical, creative skill is to spot a new opportunity and gauge whether it's worth pursuing.

So, how do people find "amazing" ideas?

For starters, we need to remember that people's perceptions about opportunities vary. As the story goes, many years ago, a shoe manufacturer sent two of his marketing graduates to Australia "to see if they could come up with new product ideas for the undeveloped aborigine market." They reported back;

"the first one said: 'There's no business here; the natives don't wear shoes of any type!' The second one responded: 'This is a great opportunity; the natives haven't even discovered shoes yet!'"[115]

So, those who spot new opportunities aren't just in the right place at the right time, they're open and ready for opportunities.

They create their own luck.

As Roman philosopher Seneca shared, "Luck is what happens when preparation meets opportunity."[116]

Creative people who have an eye for spotting new ideas follow four basic principles:[117]

1. "Notice chance opportunities"

2. "Make decisions by listening to their intuition"

3. "Create self-fulfilling prophesies via positive expectations"

4. "Adopt a resilient attitude that transforms bad luck into good"

115 John Thompson, "The World Of The Entrepreneur - A New Perspective," *Journal of Workplace Learning* 11, no. 6 (1999): 209-224.

116 Melanie Pinola, "Luck Is What Happens When Preparation Meets Opportunity," *Lifehacker*, July 19, 2013.

117 Melanie Pinola, "Luck Is What Happens When Preparation Meets Opportunity," *Lifehacker*, July 19, 2013.

In other words, you need to think like a visionary.

vi·sion·ar·y
/ˈviZHəˌnerē/

adjective

(especially of a person) thinking about or planning
the future with imagination or wisdom.

ex. "a visionary leader"[118]

Visionaries are people who can see or create opportunities
that other people may miss. What sets them apart is they are
"comfortable with ambiguity, and they can bring clarity by
piecing together previously unrelated messages and signals."[119]

MAKING SOMETHING FROM WHAT
SEEMS LIKE NOTHING

Take the company Life is Good, for example. Bert and John
Jacobs created a brand out of three words; Life is Good.

I got my first shirt from them when I was in sixth grade,
which means the shirt is more than ten years old by now. I
fell in love with the positive message. It read:

---

118 Oxford Languages, Version 12.4., s.v. "Visionary," Oxford University
Press, 2021.

119 John Thompson, "The World Of The Entrepreneur - A New
Perspective," *Journal of Workplace Learning* 11, no. 6 (1999): 209-224.

Life
is
good.

in a fun, relaxed font, very simply, right in the middle of the chest. When I got it, it was a tannish peach color with the softest fabric ever. In a sewed-on fabric box on the bottom left front corner, it read:

DO WHAT YOU LIKE.

LIKE WHAT YOU DO.

To this day, I wear the shirt as pajamas, and trust me when I say it is completely well-worn. It has so many holes in it, and this is not by any means at the fault of the creators. It has everything to do with how I took care of it when I was a kid and how often I wear the shirt now. I still refuse to throw it away, even though my sister begs me to do so profusely every day.

I fell in love with the clothing brand because of the simple message. Life is good.

I had the privilege of learning more about the company's journey while at a business convention. The company's President, Lisa Tanzer, gave a speech on her own journey to the brand. What Tanzer highlighted throughout her keynote was that they were selling a mindset. They weren't selling us anything technically unique—no new technology, limited-edition device, or exclusive product. They still don't have a revolutionary product; what they're selling is three words and the message that optimism in life is essential.

Now that is creative.

It started with two brothers, Bert and John Jacobs, from Needham, MA, just the town over from me. They had both graduated from college, and they wanted to do something artistic instead of landing a "real job" like their friends. They went out and designed a few t-shirts and decided to sell them on the streets of Boston. They bought a van called the Enterprise and decided they would travel around the country and sell their shirts. They had many conversations in the car over the summer traveling, but one of them caught their attention: how the world was filled with negative media and content. With that in the back of their minds, they continued visiting college dorms and hawking on the streets.[120]

They had to get scrappy while on the road. Sometimes they'd need to get permits to sell on the streets. Other times, they had to be creative about how they spent their money that week. With only seventy-eight dollars in their pocket at the time, they needed to be smart about what they used it on. They noted that it was weird meeting up with their friends who had chosen the more conventional route. They had full-time jobs, families, houses, and full lives. The brothers would be eating PB&J sandwiches, showering in college dorms as they traveled, and sleeping in the van most nights. Sometimes, they would splurge and grab

---

120 Natalie Walter, "The Fascinating Story of How 2 Brothers Went From Running A Failing Business Out of a Van to Building a $130 million Company," *Business Insider*, April 16, 2017.

a pizza.[121] They didn't see much success in selling their artistic shirts. They were happy if they were even able to sell one while on the streets. Instead of focusing on the negativity, though, they made sure to take lessons from every failure and success to improve their designs, colors, and sales techniques.

One night, they got together with some of their friends to show off some of their art. They put them all up on a wall and left sticky notes for people to use to leave messages. One of the drawings of a stick figure smiley face with sunglasses and a bonnet caught a girl's attention. She took a sticky and wrote that the character seemed like he had his life together. He seemed like his life was good.[122]

They saw the drawing and sticky note and decided to go for it. They printed forty-eight shirts the next day with the words "Life Is Good" and the stick figure smiley face that they later named "Jake." They went to their usual spot in Boston and set up the show. They were used to slow days and just wanted to see what people thought. In forty-eight minutes, they sold all forty-eight shirts.[123] They were shocked that they had beaten their record, and decided to continue focusing their shirts on positivity. They opened up their designs and asked what people liked to do. The brothers made shirts for people who

121 Bert Jacobs and John Jacobs, "The Life Is Good Company: Bert and John Jacobs," April 21, 2015, *How I Built This with Guy Raz*, produced by Guy Raz, podcast audio, 63:00.

122 Bert Jacobs and John Jacobs, "The Life Is Good Company: Bert and John Jacobs," April 21, 2015, *How I Built This With Guy Raz*, produced by Guy Raz, podcast audio, 63:00.

123 Natalie Walter, "The Fascinating Story of How 2 Brothers Went From Running A Failing Business Out of a Van to Building a $130 million Company," *Business Insider*, April 16, 2017.

loved hiking, biking, family, baking, and more. They found their calling: celebrate life's moments through clothing.

With more and more sales, they had money in their pockets to launch their store. They set up shop in Boston, MA, and as shirt sales increased, they started receiving letters from customers who were grateful for their work. Bert and John didn't realize the extent to which their work touched people. People going through the hardest times were grateful that the shirt was able to inspire them. For Bert and John, kids were the ultimate optimists, and many were dealing with circumstances out of their control. That's when they realized the power of optimism.[124] They created a brand focused on gratitude. Life is not easy or perfect. Life is good.

It takes a special ability to be able and spot opportunities. But it's even more unique and rare if people actually pursue the opportunity and use their skills to grow it. The best companies don't sell us products. Like Life is Good, they sell us a mission and vision for the world. They make us believe in something. And those ideas, especially, can't be rushed.

To come up with creative ideas, we need to first let ourselves be open to opportunities. Often, we are unable to find new opportunities because we're scared of change. Most people don't react well to change; we often try to resist it. As Gary Shapiro explains in his book *Ninja Innovation*, business innovation takes three forms:[125]

---

124 Ibid.

125 Gary Shapiro, *Ninja Innovation: The Ten Killer Strategies of the World's Most Successful Businesses* (New York: HarperCollins Publishers, 2015), 256.

1. **"Evolutionary"** – Everyone expects certain market improvements, for example, more powerful computer chips.

2. **"Revolutionary"** – People don't anticipate some revolutionary advances, such as smartphones' advent.

3. **"Disruptive"** – Unexpected improvements change everything, such as when mobile phones upended the landline market.

Companies can't thrive without change, and it's our responsibility to be open to change and creative opportunities.

Similarly, Michael Acton Smith was struck with a revolutionary idea while going through a difficult time. His previous company had just flopped, and he didn't know what to do. He was absolutely distraught. In his blog, he wrote:

> "There are many joys of entrepreneurial life but it can also be a chaotic, restless, and intense existence. As an entrepreneur, you're 'always on' fretting about missed opportunities and stressing about the future. By the summer of 2014, I had reached a breaking point. I was forever tired and suffered from headaches and the joy of work had faded to a dull ache."[126]

Seeing his mental health declining, his friends recommended he start meditating. Acton Smith didn't believe in meditation at first, though. He noted that he never made the time for

---

126 "Michael Acton Smith OBE," Calm, accessed March 18, 2021.

it.[127] But finally, despite his hesitancy, he started meditating, and found it helped him improve his mental state.

> "I discovered that guided meditations helped enormously and the more I practiced, the more I managed to tame my mind. I began to discover the many benefits that flow from having a strong, focused, calm mind. I felt like I'd stumbled across a secret power," he wrote.[128]

Through his personal experience, he realized meditation was more than just sitting quietly and breathing. In an interview, he explained that it's a neuroscience that helps to rewire the brain to get out of the flight or fight mindset.[129]

From there, he wondered why meditation wasn't more widespread. That's when the idea sparked. He created Calm, a meditation app, so every consumer could meditate at their own pace with an assortment of tracks.

But not many believed in it at first. "For a long time, it was an uphill battle; people didn't take us seriously," Acton Smith shared with *The Washington Post*. "They didn't think mindfulness and meditation could come via your phone or be a business."[130]

---

127 Christine Lagorio-Chafkin, "Michael Acton Smith's 'Completely Bonkers' Journey to Founding Calm, a Wellness App With a $1Billion Valuation," *Inc*, October 14, 2019.

128 "Michael Acton Smith OBE," Calm, accessed March 18, 2021.

129 Michael Acton, "Calm Co-founder: Michael Acton Smith a Pioneer in Mental Health and Wellness," October 26, 2020, *Stigma Podcast-Mental Health*, produced by Stephen Hays, podcast audio, 18:46.

130 Steven Zeitchik, "Hollywood wants to put you to sleep," *Washington Post*, November 2, 2020.

He trusted his gut, though. Having experienced the benefits of meditation firsthand, he knew the product was a revolutionary one, especially since not many had broken into the meditation space through a subscription model. In 2019, Calm hit over 40 million downloads worldwide with a new user joining every second. They have over 2 million paid subscribers and are the first unicorn startup, a privately held startup valued at over $1 billion, in meditation.[131]

Remember, to be open to the possibilities. Like the Jacobs brothers and Acton Smith, you need to be willing to try things out and trust your gut. According to Thomas Oppong, founder at AllTopStartups and author of *Working in the Gig Economy*, "To see the future with great opportunities, you must not fear experimentation or failure in this process. Opportunities always exist but you have to be able to spot them, make the most of them, dig deeper into the prospects and run with it."[132]

At the end of the day, spotting an "amazing idea" or business opportunity won't happen in the spur of the moment. It takes preparation, pure interest, and dedication. Creative people notice opportunities, choose to pursue them by listening to their gut, stay positive, and adopt a resilient attitude.

So, get out there and create your own luck.

---

131 Christine Lagorio-Chafkin, "Michael Acton Smith's 'Completely Bonkers' Journey to Founding Calm, a Wellness App With a $1Billion Valuation," *Inc*, October 14, 2019.

132 Thomas Oppong, "Ideas Are Everywhere: The Best Clues for Spotting Business Ideas," *AllTopStartups*, February 5, 2015.

9.

GO TOGETHER & GO FAR

———

As the African proverb says, "If you want to go fast, go alone. If you want to go far, go together." We've heard it time and time again; having a strong team is crucial to success in any endeavor. Businesses thrive with strong teams because teamwork helps solve problems—from collaborating with a group and brainstorming new opportunities to executing the work itself.[133] Building a great team doesn't mean you need the most brilliant people in a room together; you just need people who are interested in achieving the same goals. With driven and dedicated people from an array of experiences, we can achieve amazing results.

Sometimes, your team might be right in front of you. Think of the teams behind the beloved Ben & Jerry's or viral Furlough Cheesecake. Both teams unexpectedly started work on their companies with their best friends.

———

133 "Reason Teamwork is Important In The Workplace," *YTI*, March 26, 2015.

THE CLASSIC "TEAMWORK MAKES THE DREAM WORK"

What would you do if you showed up to work and were told you wouldn't be getting paid for weeks? What would you do if your last paycheck wasn't enough to cover costs for those weeks?

In 2018, sisters Nikki Howard and Jaqi Wright experienced this firsthand when the US government shut down for thirty-five days. Prior to the shutdown, Wright served as an analyst at the Department of Justice (DOJ) and Howard worked as a recruiter for the Food and Drug Administration (FDA).[134]

When their workplaces closed, like many furloughed workers, Howard and Wright stayed at home, waiting. Instead of stressing out about the uncertain future, Howard took to her kitchen. With no work, Howard had plenty of time to fill with baking. She started whipping up her specialty cheesecakes for her church's New Year's Eve service. When asked how they came up with their business idea, in an interview with Oprah, Wright explained that she "tapped into [her] stomach."[135]

"[My sister] saved [a cheesecake] for me that she wrapped in the fridge at home. I've had her cheesecakes before, but there was something so special about the presentation of this one and I was really excited about it," Wright shared with Oprah.[136]

---

134 Michelle Darrisaw, "How These Furloughed Sisters Used the Government Shutdown to Launch a Cheesecake Business," *Oprah Magazine*, July 31, 2019.

135 Ibid.

136 Ibid.

With every bite, Wright felt something special.

"The next day, I invited my mother to share it," Wright recalled. "After two slices, we forgot about everything. It was my mother who inspired us when she said, 'It's so good you could sell it.'"[137]

After that conversation, Wright called up her sister and said "Sissy, why don't we sell it?" Wright recalled her sister replying "Girl, I'm on furlough, and have the time, so let's go for it." They named it The Furlough Cheesecake.[138]

They started by selling cheesecakes at $29.98 and took to social media, sharing their story. In less than two weeks, they had more than 3,500 orders. Not long after, they were featured on *CNN*, *The Washington Post*, and *Ellen*. Howard and Wright had a relatable story, since 800,000 other people had also been impacted by the shutdown.[139]

"Being a woman of faith, I knew that things would be alright. But I just didn't know how they were going to work out," Howard explained.[140] "You know, when life gives you lemons,

---

137 Michelle Darrisaw, "How These Furloughed Sisters Used the Government Shutdown to Launch a Cheesecake Business," *Oprah Magazine*, July 31, 2019.

138 Nikki Howard and Jaqi Wright, "Cheesecake Business Born During Shutdown Hits Walmart," June 30, 2019, *Business*, produced by Michael Martin, podcast audio, 2:00.

139 Ibid.

140 Michelle Darrisaw, "How These Furloughed Sisters Used the Government Shutdown to Launch a Cheesecake Business," *Oprah Magazine*, July 31, 2019.

you make lemonade. So, the furlough, I think, was a catalyst to make this business come alive."[141]

They were sisters turned business partners. And they've learned so much as a team.

"My sister Jaqi has always been the one who looked out for me—and I've learned just how strong of a woman she is," Howard shared in a call with NPR, "She's not afraid to ask the questions that I'm not comfortable asking. I'm elated that I can spend time with my best friend."[142]

"Since watching this unfold, I love the fact that my little sister's been brought into the limelight," Wright chimed in. "I've really enjoyed watching her step up and step out and be bold in saying the things she wants to say. I love that she's being heard."[143]

Reflecting on their experience, Wright and Howard couldn't have predicted they'd end up working together. Think about it; your team could be right in front of you, and you just don't know it yet.[144]

Some are reluctant to bring on co-creators and co-founders, but they're key to the success of any creative endeavor. Harj

---

141 Nikki Howard and Jaqi Wright, "Cheesecake Business Born During Shutdown Hits Walmart," June 30, 2019, *Business*, produced by Michael Martin, podcast audio, 2:00.

142 Ibid.

143 Ibid.

144 Ibid.

Taggar, partner at Y Combinator, explained, "If you look at a list of the most successful startups in history, think of Apple, Facebook, Google, Microsoft, they all had co-founders when they started. And now I think sometimes people forget this point. Because when you think of these great iconic companies, you associate them with a single person, usually the CEO, who has over time risen to become prominent, famous, and a bit of a celebrity."[145]

Taggar breaks down three reasons why having a co-creator is important:

1. **Productivity.** First off, you'll be able to get more work done. But also, "if you have a co-founder who has complementary skills, they can do things that you can't." You'll get an "uplift in just the amount and quality of work you can do with a co-founder."[146]

2. **Moral support.** Starting a business is an intense and taxing process. So, it's always good to "have someone you can lean on for support during the tough times. The best co-founder relationships have this dynamic where both co-founders kind of balance each other out."[147]

3. **Pattern matching to success.** "You know, when you think of Apple, you think of Steve Jobs, when you think of Microsoft, Bill Gates, and when you think of Facebook, Mark

---

145 Harj Taggar, "How to Find the Right Co-Founder," *Y Combinator,* November 2, 2020.

146 Ibid.

147 Ibid.

Zuckerberg, right? All of these founders had co-founders. So, I think it's always important to remember that when you're starting a company and wondering whether you should have a co-founder or not."[148]

Having a strong team can make the dream possible.

Ben Cohen and Jerry Greenfield, the creators of the beloved Ben & Jerry's ice cream are another unexpected dream team. Cohen and Greenfield were childhood friends who grew up together on Long Island, New York. Like many kids, they loved ice cream. When in high school, Cohen loved it so much he even worked for an ice cream truck. After grade school, though, the two parted ways and went to college. Cohen dropped out of various colleges and instead started teaching pottery and making ice cream on a farm. Greenfield completed college and was on track to pursue medicine, but he couldn't land a spot in medical school. While the two were exploring what they wanted to pursue, they decided to go into the food business together. At first, they thought about making bagels, but they soon realized this was far too expensive and they had little knowledge of actually making them.[149]

So, instead, they turned to their love for ice cream. With very little experience, they decided to enroll in a Penn State course to learn more about how to make ice cream; the course ended up only being five dollars at the time. From there, they strategically planned to open their first store in Burlington,

148 Ibid.

149 Merrill Fabry, "Ben & Jerry's Is Turning 40. Here's How They Captured a Trend That Changed American Ice Cream," *Time*, May 4, 2018.

VT, because it was one of the few college towns without an ice cream shop. They converted a gas station to suit their ice cream parlor needs, and on May 5, 1978, they joined the ice cream scene in the US.[150]

Their first scoop was a fan favorite—with its unique chunky pieces and intensely flavored ice cream.

"I've never had a very good sense of smell, and if you don't have that, you don't have a good sense of taste. When we began, the game was for Jerry to make a flavor I could taste with my eyes closed. To do that he had to make ice creams that were intensely flavored," Cohen explained to the *New York Times*.[151]

Their teamwork led to amazing new flavors; they experimented and came up with creative options from Cherry Garcia and New York Super Fudge Chunk to Chocolate Chip Cookie Dough and Chocolate Fudge Brownie. Not all of their early ice cream flavors were successful, though. Cohen told *LIFE* that they "tried and failed with [their] first batch of Rum Raisin in 1977. It was rubbery. You put a spoon in it and the spoon pulled back." But through further experimentation, they made it work.[152]

While there were other ice cream competitors like Häagen-Dazs, Cohen and Greenfield worked to differentiate themselves. They "tried to create an image of simple-down

---

150 David Marchese,"Ben & Jerry's Radical Ice Cream Dreams," *The New York Times*, July 27, 2020.

151 Ibid.

152 Merrill Fabry, "Ben & Jerry's Is Turning 40. Here's How They Captured a Trend That Changed American Ice Cream," *Time*, May 4, 2018.

home wholesomeness."[153] They became a voice for the people—quite literally by focusing on systemic change.

In 2005, Ben & Jerry's "constructed a 900lb Baked Alaska, passing out slices on the US Capitol's lawn, in protest of oil drilling in the Arctic." In 2009, the company changed "the name of its Chubby Hubby flavor to Hubby Hubby after Vermont became the fifth state to legalize same-sex marriage." In 2016, Ben & Jerry's "hit the US Capitol again to hand out pints of Empower Mint ice cream to members of Congress along with a letter asking that they start working to reverse the Supreme Court's 2013 gutting of the Voting Rights Act."[154]

Cohen and Greenfield weren't joking about their mission; their witty ice cream titles mean far more than we think. Most recently, in 2020, Ben & Jerry's "released a statement about white supremacy and police brutality, so people can continue to tell Ben & Jerry's to 'stick to ice cream' but don't hold your breath."[155]

Through all of their time together, they never got tired of each other, and when they reflect, they explain that working together has led to the best creations.

"The most famous disagreement was about the size of the chunks in the ice cream," Greenfield shared with *The New York Times*. "Ben is well known for his inability to smell and

---

153 Ibid.

154 Caitlyn Hitt, "The Ice Cream- and Activism- Filled History of Ben & Jerry's," *Thrillist*, August 12, 2020.

155 Ibid.

therefore his inability to taste. So, he was always focused on texture in ice cream. He liked big chunks of cookies and candies. But I was the one making the ice cream, and it's hard to put big chunks in ice cream, which is why no other ice cream companies do it. I was advocating that a larger number of smaller chunks be well distributed throughout the ice cream. Ben was insisting on bigger chunks. Ben was right."[156]

According to Greenfield, both founders think Ben & Jerry's has been successful because of its "really high-quality ice cream, great ingredients, very unusual flavors — and also the activist social mission of the company." He elaborated, "Some other company could start making ice cream with big chunks the same way Ben & Jerry's does, but Ben & Jerry's having this activist, outspoken social mission — other companies can't copy that. It's not something you can just say. It has to be who the people are."[157]

After all this time in and around the ice cream business, Cohen and Greenfield have had amazing takeaways, but their most important one is:

"[Ice cream] is about happiness. Ice cream is present at most any celebration, birthday, wedding, bar mitzvah," Greenfield said. "And Americans stock ice cream in freezers as a staple."[158]

While these aren't necessarily the world's most innovative and life-changing inventions or ideas, they still required

---

156 David Marchese, "Ben & Jerry's Radical Ice Cream Dreams," *The New York Times*, July 27, 2020.

157 Ibid.

158 Ibid.

the same amount of creativity and ability to learn quickly as startups. Teamwork does, in fact, make the dream work, and sometimes your team can be right in front of you.

This is the traditional way we view teamwork, but If you think about it, teamwork means far beyond just collaborating with individuals in a room. Teamwork also includes collaborative innovation through different generations.

ANOTHER TAKE ON TEAMWORK: EMPLOYING COLLABORATIVE INNOVATION

Coming up with solutions to the world's problems or collaborating on the next innovation can be a long and tiring process. Take the Macintosh for example. US Government Engineer Douglas Engelbart showed us how to interact with computers through his innovative keyboard and "mouse" to create, edit, and move content on the screen in 1968. But Xerox really enhanced the creation through the development of the Alto personal computer. Despite this work, it was 1984 before Apple's Steve Jobs combined and transformed these developments into the Macintosh, the most innovative personal computer of its time.[159]

This is the concept of idiosyncratic innovation. While many think that innovation and creativity happens in a single event like Archimedes' "Eureka!" when he discovered the science behind levers and mechanics, it actually takes multiple moments and people to perfect and improve an idea and

---

159 Andrew Beattie, "Steve Jobs and the Apple Story," *Investopedia*, March 14, 2020.

innovation. Sometimes the perfect team ends up being made up of creatives from various moments in history.

As Greg Satell, author of *Mapping Innovation* put it, "Innovation is never a single event, and…rather than following a linear path, effective innovators combine the wisdom of diverse fields to synthesize information across domains."[160]

The power of collaborative innovation is that it helps unlock creative and disruptive ideas. New companies and those existing are mutually beneficial, according to the World Economic Forum: "Young companies profit from what older businesses already have in place: extensive networks, access to finance, organizational resources and defined processes. Conversely, established firms gain valuable insights from start-ups' novel perspectives, willingness to take risks and determination to create new, cutting-edge products."[161]

To build a successful company on innovation, we need to first understand that it takes multiple tries and a diverse set of wisdom and information to master. Creativity isn't about getting lucky either, it's about looking at ideas and inventions from different times and connecting pieces to find optimal combinations and solutions.[162] I like to think of this as the moment Tony Stark finds his father's video about the Arc Reactor. While his dad didn't have the technology to create

---

160 Greg Satell, *Mapping Innovation: A Playbook for Navigating a Disruptive Age* (New York: McGraw Hill Education, 2017), 240.

161 Martina Larkin and Derek O'Halloran, "Collaboration Between Start-ups and Corporates," *World Economic Forum* (2018): 1-21.

162 Greg Satell, *Mapping Innovation: A Playbook for Navigating a Disruptive Age* (New York: McGraw Hill Education, 2017), 240.

what he found during his time, he knew his son would have a better chance. Every time we face rejection or failure, we need to remember what happened because creativity is built on past experience and existing concepts.

Keith Sawyer, author of *Group Genius*, explained how mountain bikes were one of these "invisible collaborations." In the 1970s, cyclists in California enjoyed riding their bikes off-road and they realized their bikes couldn't really survive the rough terrain and had to be creative and quick about making repairs. One group of bikers replaced their small, narrow tires with thicker, sturdier ones while another group worked to replace their handlebars and gears. Because they all thought they were providing solutions to problems that were unique only to themselves, they never really met to collaborate. But every time one group came forward with their innovation, they were able to put them all together to create an entirely new style of bike: mountain bikes. Sometimes your "team" is around you and working on the same things you are.[163]

Take the Wright Brothers as another example. Many before had drawings of wings or devices used for flight, but the two brothers worked together to create the first functioning airplane. They used many features that were already created and put them together to fly for the first time. They first experimented with kites before moving on to gliders. They used features that were already created for gliders and combined them with a conventional engine and propeller. They were the first in the air with an engine-powered plane with their

163 Jonathan Marosz, narrator, *Group Genius: The Creative Power of Collaboration*, Keith Sawyer (audiobook), January 14, 2008, Accessed January 31, 2021.

creative mind and love for flying. Even still, there was more work to be done to make this a feasible mode of transportation. It took many more people working over generations to improve that initial creation in the commercial planes we know and use today.[164]

All of this is true for big companies as well. Companies like IBM, Procter & Gamble, Apple, Google, and Facebook require constant innovation and creativity. To be successful in creating, they need extensive research and knowledge. Companies are starting to invest more in experimenting and learning to help them improve their products and be ahead of new technological shifts.

Teamwork is crucial to the success of any creative endeavor, and it goes far beyond recruiting a team and working with them in the same room. Sometimes your "team" is made up of collaborators before and after you; after all, it can sometimes take generations of collaborative innovation to make a breakthrough. You might also be surprised where you find your collaborators and ideas. It's our job to notice innovations from other creators and find patterns and connections. Creativity isn't a straight shot; you'll need to be open to new information and experiences from others around you to create your best work.

---

164 "The Wright Brothers' Story," NASA, accessed January 31, 2021.

10.

WHAT WOULD AN ENTERTAINER DO?

———

E ntrepreneurs can learn a lot from entertainers. In fact, we should always ask ourselves *what would an entertainer do?*

Traditionally, we see entertainers as performers and artists; but entertainers have many traits in common with entrepreneurs. Good entertainers, like entrepreneurs, are skilled in four areas: they're enthusiastic, confident, adaptable, and creative. And these strengths allow entertainers to 1. tell compelling stories, 2. make the impossible seem possible, and 3. connect with their inner child—all skills that a good creator should have.

TELLING A COMPELLING STORY

Storytelling is one of the most important creative skills to have. Normally we correlate storytelling with entertainment, but it's important in all work, especially in entrepreneurship. Storytelling can be used to give speeches, presentations, host workshops, and even lead board meetings. According to Harvard Business Publishing, "telling stories is one of the most powerful means that leaders have to influence, teach, and inspire. Storytelling forges connections among people, between people and ideas."[165]

One of my favorite stories is from Matthew Luhn, a former Pixar animator. After his successful career as an animator behind works like *Toy Story*, *The Incredibles*, *Up*, and *Ratatouille*, he went on to work as a professional development coach. His most important lesson: the art of storytelling.

I was fortunate enough to see one of his talks when I was interning during my gap year. He joked that if he was going to tell us a story and tell us about the art of storytelling, then he had to be good at telling stories himself. He started by talking about his family's toy business. His father had always wanted to be an animator. Growing up, Luhn's father loved drawing and art, and one day, he mustered up the courage to tell his dad about his dream. His dad laughed it off and said that it wasn't going to happen; Luhn's grandfather planned for his father to inherit the family toy store business.

His dreams crushed, Luhn's father didn't become a Disney animator, and he ran the toy store instead. Luhn joked that, as a kid, having parents who owned a toy store was the best thing ever. "Can you imagine a kid growing up and having parents who own toy stores? You could have anything you ever wanted," Luhn shared during the session.

---

165 Vanessa Boris, "What Makes Storytelling So Effective For Learning," *Harvard Business Publishing*, December 20, 2017.

One day, when Luhn was a kid, he showed his dad a drawing he had made, "and it wasn't a good one," Luhn recalled. His dad was ecstatic; he couldn't believe his son had similar interests. With his dad's support, Luhn fell deeper in love with animation; he enjoyed creating and drawing. Beaming with pride, he went to CalArts, or "Disney's school" as Luhn put it. At CalArts, he absorbed as much as he could, but he didn't end up graduating with a degree. While in school, he was recruited to become a full-time animator. Intrigued by his work, Pixar Animations made him an offer and he took the chance.

While he was at Pixar, he was able to work on projects like *Toy Story*. Even though he was working as an animator, he loved the storytelling aspect of the film the most, specifically the anticipation of the story. In the session, he explained that if people are able to feel the emotion and anticipate, then they're even more excited to continue watching the film. Through his work, he came to understand how emotion played a part in storytelling. When we're happy, we release dopamine, which means we focus on and we remember what's happening in the story. In more somber moments, we release oxytocin which makes us more generous; we root for the hero when they're going through difficult times.

He realized later on in life that these traits weren't just important in a successful film; they were important for success in business too. He argued that there's a universal theme in life— there's always a hook. Hooks get people to act on what you're saying in a presentation; they bring out people's emotion. The reason why he transitioned to professional development after animation is because he realized the importance of emotion in business. When somebody is able to tell an effective story, they're able to bring out the emotion in someone and connect with them. Strong connection can grow into opportunity in businesses. When he realized this, he knew he needed to teach about the art of storytelling.

He talked about a movie that he worked on called *Up*. It was about Carl and Ellie. At the very beginning, and in a matter of minutes, storytellers were able to get us to cry. Through the art of storytelling, they didn't use any words at all; they used animation and music to share a story about a couple going through life together. It's clear that they were able to tell this story effectively because they understood the human emotion. They brought you on a roller coaster of feelings that made you remember the story long after it was over.

Luhn also highlighted his experience working on *The Incredibles*. To Luhn, working on presentations at work is similar to making animated films notable—they're memorable because there's an unexpected component. The art of storytelling is connecting pieces together and making things unexpected. So, when they came up with *The Incredibles*, they thought, *Okay, what are superheroes created for?* Superheroes are created for saving people's lives. *What would happen if a superhero, or superheroes were banned?*

Your first thought might be, *Why are superheroes banned if they save people?* You want to know more. This is the art of anticipation, and it's effective in business. By making your audience—clients or investors—sit on the edge of their seats in anticipation, you engage with them in a more impactful way than leading them through bleak slides. Introducing exciting innovations and ideas with a story reaches them in a way numbers and Key Performance Indicators (KPIs) can't. They connect with them emotionally.

Another example of anticipation is the concept behind *Ratatouille—What if a rat loved to cook?* They wanted to mix two things that were really controversial: rats and kitchens. The stories are so unique, but you're able to relate with characters like Remy because he goes through the same themes of life that we do. He's just trying to pursue his passion and do what he loves.

Storytelling, like many other skills that seem mundane, is crucial to creative thinking and finding new ideas. In entrepreneurship, it's important to communicate your thoughts and experiences clearly. So, Pixar animators and entrepreneurs have a lot more in common than we think. When you have an idea for your business, there will be a story for it. An entrepreneur's job is to share that story with customers and stakeholders. As the podcast *Get Storied* put it, "Creativity and storytelling are like Oreos and milk—separate, they're nice, but together they're magic."[166] The only way to effectively share an idea is to tell it through a story.

MAKING THE IMPOSSIBLE, POSSIBLE
"If you're really doing something worthwhile I think you will be pushed to the brink of hopelessness before you come through the other side"

- *GEORGE LUCAS*

---

166 Michelle James, "Storytelling and the Creative Process," November 25, 2018, *Storytelling and the Creative Process*, produced by Michael Margolis, podcast audio, 1:53:00.

Entertainers make the impossible, possible—often by being adaptable. And this is a key trait for all entrepreneurs. While working on a new venture, entrepreneurs need to be able to adapt quickly to changes. Sometimes funding falls through or the product doesn't work, and it's an entrepreneur's responsibility to pick up the pieces and make what seems impossible possible, just like entertainers.

I am a huge *Star Wars* fan. I've seen every movie, almost every animated show or movie, and every TV show. Like the entire fan base, I fell in love with it because of the fantastical world and journey. Today, I can't imagine a world without *Star Wars*.

So how did Lucas create this brand that everyone around the world adores? Well to start, he didn't intend to go into movie making; initially, he wanted to be a race car driver. As fate would have it, he found himself in a near-fatal accident days before his high school graduation and as a result, he went to community college to study Cinematography instead. Another opportunity presented itself there; his friend recommended he transfer to a school with even more movie creation resources, which led him to move to the University of Southern California. He worked tirelessly on various projects, having found what he loved.

Not everything was a success, though. He hit a few flops like his first dystopian film *THX 1138*, but he didn't lose hope. He started work on another film, *American Graffiti*, which earned five academy awards. He found success with this work because he combined his love for cars and cinematography.[167]

---

167 Ba Myint, "George Lucas and the Origin Story Behind 'Star Wars,'" *Biography*, October 14, 2020.

From there, he created a fantasy and adventure story that would take place in an imaginary outer space, also known as the beloved *Star Wars*. While people were skeptical, Lucas was able to convince an executive at 20th Century Fox with his two-page synopsis of the plot, idea, and characters. That was all he needed: someone to believe. And his work blew people away. He found a way to creatively combine new technology with fantasy, by which many were amazed. The films were made with so much detail from the special effects, unique character costumes, beautiful sets and scenery, and a heartfelt yet comedic plot. Lucas used his creative imagination to ensure entertainment for all ages. Parents and kids lined up for miles outside of movie theaters to watch the film, which grossed over $513 million from an $11 million budget.[168]

He didn't stop there, though. After the success of his first film, he got to work on the second and third. He was determined to keep his stories in trilogies; in his mind, that was the only way to do it. He needed to continue growing in order to make the films he envisioned. Lucas put his attention toward special effects and ensuring they had the technology needed to make his concepts come to life; he created Industrial Light & Magic and Skywalker Sound. His new technology—from how we film effects and create fantasy sets—continues to play a role in today's films and has set the stage for even more innovators to create resources needed to make film concepts become a reality.[169]

His ideas created multiple companies. His storyline created a brand. His brand created a world. And all of it came from

168 Ibid.

169 Ibid.

his creativity, curiosity, and love for cinematography and storytelling. Throughout all of it, Lucas had to be scrappy. He needed to find ways to make the technology; he needed to find a way to raise the money he needed; he needed to get the rights to the company; and he needed to find a way to make his dream become a reality.

Lucas is the epitome of an adaptable entertainer: someone who is willing to roll with the punches to reach their goal. And his ability to adapt quickly helps him make the impossible possible, through innovative film technology and creative fundraising.

Take it from the company known for creativity. The Walt Disney Company has done amazing work, keeping to their mission and brand while also making a name for themselves in all areas of entertainment. It's always incredible to see how Walt Disney created the company through his imagination, and I've been particularly drawn to how he created the beloved Disney Parks. There are plenty of videos of Disney working on the plans for Disneyland and in many documentaries, he can be seen walking through an empty field in Anaheim setting things up. Disney was someone who could see the future and could convince others to see his vision too.[170]

While watching the creation of Disneyland is exciting for any Disney lover, the story itself is so amazing and magical, especially watching Walt overcome his own doubt and others' doubt. He's was told "no" over and over again, but he adapted and kept going. Most notably, he created a team

---

170 *DisneyPlus*, "The Imagineering Story," November 12, 2019, video, 69:00.

of creators called the Imagineers, to help him shape what seemed unattainable.

Most of the Imagineers were movie creators, so working on a theme park was a little outside of their wheelhouse. But this meant they thought outside the box when it came to working on rides, effects, and settings. They saw Disneyland as a place where everyone was their own camera person, and they wanted to make sure every angle of the take told a story and made people happy. What they planned didn't seem possible, but they found a way to make it possible because they were creative.[171]

For example, Bob Gurr, an Imagineer, came on the team because he worked on cars and Disney told him he wanted him to create his own car for the Autotopia ride. After working on the ride, Disney had him work on a variety of other projects around the park, which most definitely weren't within his realm. He worked on creating a moving and talking Abe Lincoln. He also worked on creating one of the most iconic roller coasters: the Matterhorn Bobsleds. Every member of Disney's team was quick on their feet and able to adjust when needed. They weren't your usual business leaders, but they helped build one of the most successful theme parks and brands in the world.[172]

Walt Disney was ahead of his time. Those working on the park explained that he would come in to see how they were doing, and he would ask why another piece wasn't done. He

171 Ibid.
172 Ibid.

wasn't satisfied with what was done yesterday; he was always looking toward the future.[173]

So, think like an entertainer and perhaps you can also make the seemingly impossible, possible. From an entrepreneurial standpoint, Disney and Lucas highlight the importance of being adaptable and sticking with your dream. You too can make the impossible possible. So, think like an entertainer.

BEING A KID AGAIN

Entertainers often look to kids for inspiration, and some say they know they are moving in the right direction on a project when they "feel like a kid again."

Take film composers for example. It's not easy becoming a film composer; for starters, they need to absolutely love movies and music because they can spend months working on compositions for different projects. In addition, like a business, they need to be strong in communication, sales, project management, team building, networking, and time management. They also need to come up with the actual composition and arrangements.

I've always loved movie soundtracks. Growing up, I actually fell in love with many movies because of their soundtracks. They put all of the content into perspective and set the tone for each scene throughout the movie. Music in film adds the final touches on the project and pushes the audience to feel what the hero or characters are feeling. They make us sense

---

173 Ibid.

what visuals alone wouldn't be able to accomplish. Music can help build suspense when the hero is in danger, make us emotional at the end of the story, and can fill us with anticipation or excitement at critical moments in a film. As acclaimed director Brad Bird stressed, "If the music isn't right, it can really ruin all of the other work that's been done. If it's great, it takes it and multiplies it by five."[174]

Michael Giacchino, a notable film composer known for his work on *The Incredibles, War for the Planet of the Apes, Ratatouille, Star Trek, Jurassic World, Rogue One: A Star Wars Story, Coco, Up, Inside Out,* and more, employs his inner child regularly.[175]

Before becoming a mega-composer, Giacchino started by making films in his basement when he was a teenager. Early on, he realized his love for creating music for films; it was his favorite part of creating his personal movies. He loved the process. He didn't realize it at the time, but the best composers fully immersed themselves in their work and relied on knowledge from previous composers to inspire new creations. In his case, he spent his childhood in his dad's basement shuffling through vinyl. His love for music and strong exposure to it set the base for his musical ability.[176]

I've always found the creative process for composing music interesting. How does someone go about creating the

174 *Pixar Post*, "Incredibles 2 Scoring Session B-Roll & Michael Giacchino & Brad Bird Interview," June 7, 2018, video, 4:46.

175 "Michael Giacchino," Michael Giacchino, accessed January 30, 2021.

176 Helen O'Hara, "Film Studies 101: Michael Giacchino On Being A Composer," *Empire Online*, May 30, 2014.

soundtrack for feature films? For "Married Life" from the Pixar film *Up*, Giacchino came up with the song while in the shower. For weeks, Pete Docter, the director of *Up*, told him he was looking for a track that sounded like something someone could hear if they opened up a box in their grandma's house. While he had a few ideas, Giacchino still hadn't found *the one*, but on what was a regular day, the tune just came to him. As soon as he got out of the shower, he started playing it on the piano. But, instead of writing it down right away, Giacchino told himself he'd wait until tomorrow and see if he still remembered it. If it was still in his head the next day, he'd take it to the director as an idea.[177] Sure enough, it stuck, and he presented the tune to the director who replied, "That's the one!"[178]And the made-in-the-shower track landed Giacchino an Oscar, Golden-Globe, BAFTA, and two Grammys.

This was only the start.

The first scene Giacchino composed for *Up* was "Married Life," and it was pretty complicated. While he had the tune, he had to make sure he was able to tell a very emotional story. For Giacchino, it went beyond just scoring for a Pixar film; the music was the emotion that motivated him to create one of his most powerful works. Even after recording it and being happy with the product, Giacchino knew they could do better. Months after recording the final, they got back to work fixing errors that would help the music and the scene flow better.

177 Helen O'Hara, "Film Studies 101: Michael Giacchino On Being A Composer," *Empire Online*, May 30, 2014.

178 Ibid.

They even had the animation team work on editing the scene to go better with the music.[179]

Giacchino absolutely loves what he does, and you can tell when you hear his music. He takes the time to make sure every detail fits perfectly, and he doesn't just pick any film to work on. He looks for projects that excite him. Even with a ton of experience up his sleeve, it's still important that he connects with the material.

> "I want them to be, first of all, projects that I'm passionate about. And second of all, projects that the people I'll be spending a lot of time with are people that I actually like spending time with. So much of it is about who the director is. Is it somebody that I feel I can get along with? That's important to me when I spend so much time working on these things. If you look at my credits, most of them are the same directors over and over. It's like your group of friends when you were growing up, your core group of friends. The guys I work with all grew up loving movies and listening to film scores so you're speaking this crazy geek language, these weird facts that nobody else knows. There's not a lot of directors who can name the soundtrack to *Airport '77* in the way JJ will pull that out. It's great because I'll know exactly what he's talking about," he shared.[180]

---

179 Ibid.

180 Ibid.

And when he works with the people he loves on material he loves, he feels like a kid again.

"I always tell JJ that it's really fun when we work together because it really does feel like we're ten again. We're literally saying to each other, 'Oh my god, wouldn't it be so cool if we did this?' in the same way that when you were a kid you'd be like, 'Wouldn't it be great if we made a robot?' And you make a robot out of trash cans and it doesn't work. You made something and it was fun and that's what I look for when I'm working," he said.[181]

Composers, like businesspeople, need constant collaboration and inspiration. What makes the most successful entertainers and creative people is their love for finding projects that excite them and willingness to fully immerse themselves in their work like kids when they play. Composers and executives aren't too different after all. To succeed in any creative endeavor, you need to embrace your inner kid.

* * *

So, before jumping into a major creative project, always ask yourself:

What would an entertainer do?

Entertainers are enthusiastic, confident, adaptable, and creative; they are strong in storytelling, make the impossible

---

181 Ibid.

possible, and embrace being a kid at heart. A great entertainer understands human nature, stays positive, and oozes confidence. There's a lot that entrepreneurs can learn from entertainers; and we need to incorporate those skills into our creative work.

PART 4

THE POWER OF CREATIVITY

11.

PATIENCE IS YOUR PAL

———

I magine you have $5,000 in your bank account, you've just finished college, and you've failed the LSAT more times than you'd like to count. After what seemed to be your biggest failure, you decide to audition for a role at Disney as a performer. Instead of getting a princess, the character you hoped to get, you're told to be a chipmunk. After failing yet again, you decided to sign up and become a fax machine salesperson. At this point, you're used to getting told "no" again and again. While on a sales trip, you find yourself sweating up a storm and would prefer to have something that keeps your tummy tucked and butt curved without restraining your legs and feet, so you decide to cut holes into your tights to make them more comfortable and breathable. Now, you're able to keep the figure but also wear your super cute shoes.

That's it! You found it!

Always looking for ways to improve and solve problems, you look into creating your own brand of these pantyhose because you've found them so helpful. You message a few friends and go into a store to ask someone what they think about this problem and solution. You spend hours sorting through the library researching trademarks and how you can actually create this product. Once you figure out how to make your invention, you head over to the manufacturers with your idea. You go from head to head, asking them if they can help you create this product.

Their answer: no.

This is what Sara Blakely, founder and CEO, went through when founding and creating her company SPANX.[182] This is also a glimpse of the process many other innovators go through when trying to share their solution to a simple and common situation to better people's lives. In many of her speeches, Blakely highlights how the process wasn't an easy one. She was the designer, creator, publicist, operations manager, salesperson, etc. and she had to learn how to do everything as she went along. I find this story so inspiring because Blakely found a way to make her dream and product work. In fact, she's one of the few self-made female billionaires.[183] Blakely had what many are sometimes scared to own: hard work and perseverance. She went all in on her work and acted as all of the key players in founding and getting the company off the ground despite constantly being told no.[184]

---

182 Sara Blakely, "How Spanx Got Started," *Inc*, January 20, 2012.

183 Gillian Segal, "This Self- Made Billionaire Failed The LSAT Twice, Then Sold Fax Machines For 7 Years Before Hitting Big-Here's How She Got There," *CNBC*, April 3, 2019.

184 *MasterClass*, "MasterClass Live with Sara Blakely," June 18, 2020, video, 1:01:37.

Her story speaks volumes about the society we live in today. Commonly, business is seen as a glamorous profession. Many misconceptions around entrepreneurs include "entrepreneurs are wealthy," "entrepreneurs work from the beach and Starbucks a few hours a day," and "entrepreneurs just need one good idea to be successful."[185] When we talk about business success stories, we often gloss over the person's creativity, resilience and, most importantly, their patience. What we can learn from Blakely is how to be patient and keep trying regardless of setbacks, and instead, use those setbacks to reflect in order to grow in the future.

According to historian, art critic, and author Christopher Jones, patience is the unsung hero of creativity. It's important to "ride rejection and [wait] for success." Jones likes to think about it this way: "With every rejection, I've come to identify an opportunity to think afresh about the work. Was it really as good as I thought it was? Invariably I ask myself this question and the answer is usually 'No'. Thankfully, with the rejection, I have another chance to improve the work. Iteration by iteration the piece steadily improves, and — rather like moving through the gears of a car — the power and potential of the work builds."[186]

Another woman who has shown great patience and resilience is my aunt, Sheila Lirio Marcelo, or Tita Sheila.

---

185 Jonathan Long, "Starting A Business Does Not Mean You're Your Own Boss, and Other Misconceptions About Being An Entrepreneur," *Business Insider*, October 8, 2015.

186 Christopher Jones, "Patience is the Unsung Hero of Creativity," *Christopher P Jones*, May 10, 2019.

She grew up in the Candelaria Province in the Philippines with my dad and their four other siblings. Growing up, I always heard stories about how my grandparents ventured out into different businesses—from running chicken farms to generating energy from coconuts. My family had a strong entrepreneurial background and mindset. They were always driven and ambitious.

When it came time to attend college, my aunt, dad, and their siblings had the amazing opportunity to attend in the US. My aunt attended Mount Holyoke College, a historically women's college in Western Massachusetts; she excelled in classes and majored in Economics. When she was in her twenties, though, she hit a snag; she was pregnant with her first child, my cousin Ryan. I can't fathom what she went through at the time while working to complete school and raise a newborn. She was worried about her career; the whole family was. She thought this would be a major setback and derail her plans to go to law school. Instead, she got back to work, married my uncle Tito Ron, and persisted through.

Despite the challenges, she graduated Mount Holyoke with honors and went into the workforce. After gaining some professional experience, she pushed through to pursue her MBA and JD like she had planned at Harvard University. She worked long hours studying for two degrees, and while in grad school, she welcomed another bundle of joy into the world, my other cousin, Adam. While sitting down with her after dinner, she recounted memories of her trying to study while getting the minimal amount of sleep to function. Not to mention, my uncle Tito Ron was also pursuing his MBA at Harvard. Not only did they have to manage a household of four and classes, but they also had to work to put food on the table. After grad school, she continued to gain more experience in consulting and working with other tech companies.

Her biggest career move was founding and serving as CEO and Chairwoman of Care.com, which she created due to her own personal difficulty finding care for her two sons and balancing the dynamic of having to take care of one's parents and children.

My aunt is a great example of the power of patience. Without becoming a mother at an early age, the idea probably wouldn't have come to her. But she didn't know that then. In the moment, she was stressed, worried, and uncertain about the future. She had no idea that she would become one of the few female CEOs to bring a company public either. Not only did she found and lead the company for thirteen years, she also scaled it and brought it public. She could've overstressed and gotten bogged down, but instead was patient. According to *Psychology Today*, "Practicing patience will help you dissipate stress and give you a choice about how you respond to disappointment and frustration. When you can stay calm, centered, and not act rashly out of frustration, all areas of your life will improve."[187]

While we've glamorized the business world, I can attest and say it is not an easy process. After shadowing and working alongside my aunt for years, I understand the patience and grit necessary to succeed in the world of entrepreneurship.

---

187 Judith Orloff, "The Power of Patience" *Psychology Today*, September 18, 2012.

Even when you have an idea that can help improve the world, people will always work against you or stand in the way. She worked long hours and fought for years to make her dream a reality.

I aspire to follow in her footsteps in business because I love being part of projects that start with a small idea and grow based on the work and commitment you put into them. She's taught me that anything is possible as long as you have patience and resilience. If you ever work with her, you'll see how much she loves what she does. She does her work with purpose and she's patient with her goals. She always reflects on her past work and is conscious about how it has gotten her where she is today.

Both my aunt and Blakely found their creative solutions by going through challenges themselves. Blakely was unhappy with her undergarments and wanted to make a change to help other women struggling with the same challenges, and my aunt was struggling to make work and life balance out while she pursued her career. Both women took on problems that they faced and found a way to help others going through the same. And through the process, they were patient. They understood that creating and problem solving wouldn't happen overnight, and they knew it would take a lot of work and learning. Patience is an underrated force of creativity, and the best creators are patient with the work that they're doing.

12.

BELIEVE & YOU'RE
HALFWAY THERE

W e've all heard the saying, "If you don't believe in yourself, no one else will." It's an imperative part to mastering creativity, because if you don't think you're going to succeed, how will anyone else believe you will?

The first thing is to believe that your idea, concept, or passion will succeed, and you have to trust it. When you do believe in yourself, you also build your own self-confidence. If you have confidence in yourself, you're more likely to push yourself and find inspiration to take action. If you have low self-confidence or don't believe you can actually do something, you'll have very little motivation to actually put in the full force of your effort.

Having a positive and confident attitude is crucial to success. As Winston Churchill put it "Attitude is a little thing that makes a big difference."[188] If you don't believe that it's going to work out and you're very pessimistic about how you're going about it or have a lot of self-doubt, then clearly, it won't work. Positivity and belief are key. But, in addition to being positive and believing in yourself, you also have to understand that failure is part of the process; it's something you can learn from, and the feeling of loss is only temporary. Because after every failure, you'll be able to learn from it and move forward. You'll be able to become your most creative self by believing in your own abilities, knowledge, and capabilities to create what you want.

According to psychologist Albert Bandura, research conducted on self-efficacy suggests that building on your past successes is key to believing in your own ability to achieve.[189] So focus on what you've achieved and see how you've gotten where you are today.

BELIEVE IN YOURSELF

When you find that belief in yourself and have the confidence to achieve the things you want, you'll find that brilliant ideas can come at any time. Take the creator Richard Montañez of Flamin' Hot Cheetos for instance.

My little sister loves Flamin' Hot Cheetos. Every time I go to CVS or the grocery store, she asks if she can come. Not because she wants to accompany me, but because she wants

---

188 Winston Churchill, "Attitude is A Little Thing That Makes a Big Difference," *BrainyQuote*, accessed January 31, 2020.

189 Albert Bandura, *Self-Efficacy Mechanism in Human Agency*, Volume 37, no. 2 (1982): 122-147.

to buy Cheetos. I was shocked to find that everyone in my college seemed to love them too. It was one of the most consistent snacks to show up at parties or kickbacks, and some of my friends even had a tradition of eating Hot Cheetos with pickles pretty regularly.

With how popular and widespread Hot Cheetos are now, it's pretty amazing to learn how the product came to be. I heard the story during a late-night study session with a friend and was so intrigued that I had to learn more.

Montañez, a former janitor in one of the Frito-Lay California plants, came up with the idea for Flamin' Hot Cheetos completely by chance and made it happen because of his belief in himself. He started working as a janitor at Frito-Lay when he was eighteen or nineteen, and he was really curious to learn more. He asked a salesman if he could accompany him on his trips during his day off. The salesman agreed because it was free labor for him, and Montañez saw it as a great opportunity to explore and learn. He got up at 5 a.m. on his day off to help load the trucks and get on the road to vendors. He learned about how they talked about the product and what they offered. Early on, he noticed how they didn't have many options catering to Latinos.[190]

He recalls a day when he was in his house and the "*elote* man*" came through town as usual selling *elote*, a Mexican "street corn." Montañez ordered one and watched the man put chili powder, salt, cotija, lime juice, and crema fresca

---

190 Andrew Whalen, "The True Story OF the Flamin' Hot Cheetos Inventor Richard Montañez," *Newsweek*, August 27, 2019.

on the cob, and he took a bite. With the bite, he realized it looked like a Cheeto. He thought, *What if I put chili on a Cheeto?* He went back into the house and called his wife. He said, "We need to make these!" While he didn't know much about the product, he knew there was something missing—they weren't utilizing spices. He went to the factory and took naked Cheetos home, and he and his wife started experimenting with spices in their kitchen to get the perfect recipe. Once they had a few options, they started bringing them to parties for people to try, and everyone loved them.[191]

Montañez knew he couldn't stop there. He had found something that Frito-Lay was missing and was determined to share the idea with the company. Having very little experience and exposure in the business world, Montañez ended up doing something no other employee would dare to do. He grabbed the company phonebook and looked up CEO Roger Enrico's contact information. Looking back, Montañez noted that he didn't know what he should've done during the process; he just knew he needed to share the idea with someone, and the CEO made the most sense. "I was naïve," Montañez said. "I didn't know you weren't supposed to call the CEO...I didn't know the rules." He dialed the number and got in touch with the executive assistant. He told her that he needed to schedule a meeting to make a pitch. The assistant asked, "Ok. What division are you with?"[192]

---

191 *OMAR ELATTAR & THE PASSIONATE FEW*, "Janitor Who Created Hot Cheetos: Amazing Life Story Interview! (Must Watch)," October 6, 2017, video, 1:42:10.

192 Ibid.

"I'm in California," he replied.

"You're a VP for California?"

"No. I work at the Rancho Cucamonga plant."

"Oh, you're the VP of Operations?"

"No, I work in the plant."

"Ok. You're the plant manager?"

"No. I'm the janitor."

He was on hold for a bit and then someone picked up the phone again, "Hello, this is Roger."[193]

Montañez couldn't believe his luck. He briefly went over the details of his idea and the CEO loved his passion and excitement. Before ending the call, he said, "I'll be at the plant in two weeks. I'd love to hear more. Please prepare a presentation."

He couldn't forget the days leading up to meeting the CEO. At the time, Montañez couldn't read and write very well and didn't have much knowledge on how to create a business proposal, but he wasn't going to let that stop him. He and his wife headed to the library in search of marketing information, and then he made sure to have the product ready for sampling. They filled 100 plastic bags with homemade Hot

---

193 *OMAR ELATTAR & THE PASSIONATE FEW,* "Janitor Who Created Hot Cheetos: Amazing Life Story Interview! (Must Watch)," October 6, 2017, video, 1:42:10.

Cheetos and manually drew the logo and design on each bag. He walked into the CEO's room and gave him the pitch he had prepared; Roger loved it. Shortly after, Montañez found himself signing papers to become a VP at Frito-Lay to oversee the new Hot Cheetos brand.[194]

Through this experience, Montañez learned a really important life lesson: everyone has something to offer the world. He believes, "All you need is one revelation to create a revolution." He didn't know it at the time, but he had an amazing idea to share with the world that ended up becoming a multibillion-dollar snack.[195]

Montañez was presented with a creative opportunity and went with it. To this day, he tells young people to stay open-minded because you never know what you might find. For Montañez, he was able to successfully create a new product line because of the belief he had in his own abilities and ideas.[196]

BELIEVING IN YOUR PRODUCT AND TEAM

In addition to believing in yourself, you need to believe in your product and team. Hamdi Ulukaya, founder and CEO of Chobani, took this approach.

Ulukaya's story not only speaks volumes about the importance of believing in one's product and team, but it also

---

194 Ibid.

195 Andrew Whalen, "The True Story OF the Flamin' Hot Cheetos Inventor Richard Montañez," *Newsweek*, August 27, 2019.

196 *OMAR ELATTAR & THE PASSIONATE FEW*, "Janitor Who Created Hot Cheetos: Amazing Life Story Interview! (Must Watch)," October 6, 2017, video, 1:42:10.

highlights the importance of remaining humble and giving back whenever possible. Ulukaya, originally a small cheese shop owner, grew up in Turkey with his parents who made cheese and yogurt.[197]

While in the US, he noticed a lack of quality yogurt in grocery stores. That's when he knew he found a need, and despite his dislike of business, he started to look into purchasing a factory to start his yogurt company. He received a flyer in the mail that said, "Fully equipped yogurt plant for sale."[198]

At first, he hesitated, but then he decided to take the drive to upstate New York to check it out. The dilapidated Kraft plant was eighty-five years old and in the midst of closing due to budget cuts and their own exit from the yogurt market due to low sales. When he visited, he noticed the chipping painted walls and the sour milk stench, but he saw far more than just a broken-down building. He saw potential that no one else could see, especially in the employees. Ulukaya recalls fifty-five employees working to shut the factory down while he visited. With his creativity, passion, and drive, he saw the bright future of an amazing company, which would start with creating the best yogurt.[12]

As soon as he saw the factory, he called his lawyer to make the deal. His lawyer wasn't as thrilled as Ulukaya was though, especially as Ulukaya didn't have enough money to finance the project. That fact didn't bother Ulukaya though. He was

197 *Chobani*, "Hamdi Ulukaya, Chobani Founder's Story," April 8, 2013, video, 1:32.

198 Hamdi Ulukaya, "The Anti-CEO Playbook," Lecture, TED, 2019.

determined to start his business and took out a few loans to make it possible. A few months later, he had the factory he needed. Once he had the factory, the second step was to hire four of the fifty-five original employees left. At first, they were all hesitant. Why did Ulukaya believe he could pull this off when Kraft, one of the most well-known dairy companies, was closing their factory? Despite their uncertainty, they followed his lead. Their first project: repaint the factory![199] The employees asked what other plans he had, and Ulukaya said he wasn't sure at the time. He likes to imagine he'd said something like this to his team:

"See these walls we're painting? In two years, we're going to launch a yogurt here that Americans have never seen and never tasted before. It will be delicious; it will be natural. And we're going to call it 'Chobani'—it means 'shepherd' in Turkish. We are going to hire all of the fifty-five employees back, or most of them back. And then one hundred more after, and then one hundred more after, and then one thousand more after that. You see that town over there? Every person we hire, ten more local jobs will be created. The town will come back to life, the trucks will be all over the roads. And the first money we make, we're going to build one of the best Little League baseball fields for our children. And five years after that, we're going to be the number one Greek yogurt brand in the country."[200]

He now jokes, "Would they have believed me? Of course not. But that's exactly what happened."[201]

---

199 Ibid.

200 Hamdi Ulukaya, "The Anti-CEO Playbook," Lecture, TED, 2019.

201 Ibid.

This story in itself is amazing. Ulukaya started with a simple goal: "paint the walls and we'll take it from there." He believed in his product and in his team to bring his ambition to life. It was a challenging process, though. He had to create the recipe that people would love. He needed to come up with a cup design that would grab people's attention in the store. He needed to creatively find ways to place his product in notable stores around the country.

Ulukaya loves telling the story about how his product ended up in its first few grocery stores. When they first made Chobani and finally created the final product, they shipped their first two hundred cases out to a customer on Long Island. He had been working with his team tirelessly for two years to perfect the yogurt and cups, and they were so excited for their shipment. He recalls the week he waited to hear about the sale was the longest in his life. He waited anxiously to hear whether or not there was good news or bad news about the product's performance. It was their first time seeing how the product would be out in the world. He finally had time to breath once he called the store owner to see what had happened.[202]

They had good news. People were attracted to the cup the team designed and kept picking it up, but Ulukaya wanted to know more.[203]

"Is it the same people buying it or are more people? It's important for me to know."[204]

---

202 Ibid.

203 Ibid.

204 Ibid.

The store owner said it was the same people buying, but they were telling people they knew about it too. To his relief, the store owner purchased more, as the product showed success. Ulukaya knew this was a good sign. He wasn't dancing and partying yet, but he knew things were looking up.[205]

A few weeks after they got into another store, Ulukaya told his team, "Let's go to a big store! Chain stores." His team told him it wasn't possible. If they wanted to be on those shelves, they had to shell out money that they didn't have. That didn't stop Ulukaya. He met with the store owner of ShopRite and talked to them about his product.[206]

They had their five flavors at the time—strawberry, blueberry, peach, vanilla, and plain—that they wanted to put on the shelf. ShopRite replied, "That's $200,000." That was $200,000 the company didn't have at the time. What Ulukaya told them: "We promise this is going to sell."[207]

The store owner laughed; Ulukaya chuckles at this story to this day because he still can't believe it. He told them, "We promise this is going to sell, and every week, we can cut 10 percent for the $200,000." The store owner, at this point was profusely laughing, said, "What if it doesn't sell?" Ulukaya's response: "We're going to give you the factory." The store owner laughed even further, but he also liked the team's positivity and decided to give them a chance.[208]

---

205 Ibid.

206 Ibid.

207 Hamdi Ulukaya, "The Anti-CEO Playbook," Lecture, TED, 2019.

208 Ibid.

Ulukaya motions with his hands to show where their yogurt was located in the dairy aisle. Dominated by Yoplait and Dannon, Chobani was located in the upper right corner of the yogurt shelf. He recalls having to really look for the cups on the shelf. So, Ulukaya's next goal: create a cup that caught people's attention even more so. He sleeved them, and he created the graphic and everything; when people walked by the aisle, you couldn't miss Chobani.[209]

A few weeks later, the store owner called with an update. It was good news. He said, "I don't know what crap you put in this cup. Do not tell me." In that moment, Ulukaya knew the team was doing something right. People found the yogurt addictive and kept coming back for more. He realized that making a strong product he believed in was far more important than just selling one.[210] Soon after, Ulukaya moved into the factory and got to work to continue to improve the product and create something worthy of the people.

For Ulukaya, his company is far more than just yogurt. He wanted to change the world. Today, he continues to help and spread awareness on the refugee cause, he teaches entrepreneurs about the importance of giving back and valuing individual employees, and he leads as America's number one Greek yogurt. You'll find it in any grocery or convenient store and can even grab some at flagship stores in major cities. His idea was a simple one. He wanted to create the best yogurt in America. He never took business courses or went to business school and he never worked for a major corporation. He just

---

209 Ibid.

210 Ibid.

had his creativity, family background, positivity, passion, and people who believed in him. That's all he needed to lead a successful food company.

"The treasure that I found in that factory—dignity of work, strength of character, human spirit—is what we need to unleash all across the world."[211]

Ulukaya's lesson teaches us something important in every facet of our lives. Unless you live a magical life, you, as a creative businessperson, need to get used to failure. Positive and resilient entrepreneurs and creators seek new paths if their current one isn't possible. That's what Ulukaya did. He continued to look for new solutions to problems facing his business to get his product out in the world, and he believed wholeheartedly in his product and team. Belief in what you're doing is key in succeeding as a creative and as a businessperson. The road is a tough one, but you have to stick through it and watch your creativity pay off. Ulukaya believed in himself, in his team, and in his product.

Successful products like Hot Cheetos and Chobani were created by *someone*, so why can't that someone be you? All you need to do is believe in yourself and what you're working on. Once you do, you're halfway there!

---

211 *Chobani*, "Hamdi Ulukaya, Chobani Founder's Story," April 8, 2013, video, 1:32.

13.

REFLECT SO YOU DON'T REPEAT

———

C reativity relies on the ability to reflect, reconnect, and refocus.

As we go through work, we sometimes lose track of what we're doing and why we're doing it. When you lose that initial motivation and initial spark of creativity, you lose your message and direction. The most creative people reflect on their work to continue iterating, improving, and growing. So, every time you succeed or fail, you need to reflect on the moment and look backwards to learn about the future.

According to executive coach Jennifer Porter,

"Reflection gives the brain an opportunity to pause amidst the chaos, untangle and sort through observations and experiences, consider multiple possible interpretations, and create meaning."[212]

UNDERSTANDING YOUR PRIORITIES

When you understand what your priorities are you're able to be your most creative self. Often, we lose track of our priorities when we get too engulfed in work; consequently, we lose our creative edge.

Taylor Swift reignites her creativity by reflecting on her priorities often. Throughout her career, she's reflected on her music and how it's changed through the years. Each album—*Taylor Swift, Fearless, Speak Now, Red, 1989, Reputation, Lover, Folklore,* and *Evermore*— is a reflection of what she was going through at the time.

"There is an element to my fan base where we feel like we grew up together. I'll be going through something, write the album about it, and then it'll come out. And sometimes, it'll coincide with what they're going through, kind of like they're reading my diary," she said in her *Miss Americana* documentary.[213]

Early on, Swift recognized her niche in music: storytelling through songwriting. Without it, she noted, she wouldn't be where she is today.

Through the years in the spotlight, she started reflecting on how she ended up becoming one of the biggest artists in

---

212 Jennifer Porter, "Why You Should Make Time for Self-Reflection (Even If You Hate Doing It)," *Harvard Business Review,* March 21, 2017.

213 Lana Wilson, director, *Miss Americana,* Netflix Original Film, 2020.

the music business. Going through old diaries, she noticed a trend: she always wanted to appear good and fit the mold of a model young girl. When she reached her twenties, she recognized how this mindset affected her own growth as an adult. Her entire life, she filled her insecurities and voids with clapping, acceptance, and approval from the media, her fans, and the general public. When she was young, she didn't realize the toll it took on her mental health and ability to be her best self.[214]

"I really just went to this place where I was like, 'I'm going to prove myself. I'm going to make sure people know I deserve to be here.'"[215]

She finally realized she hit rock bottom when she met her "life goal"—winning Album of the Year at the Grammys for the second time. She never thought it was possible, but when it happened, she was in shock.

"I remember thinking afterward 'Oh my god, that was all you wanted. That was all you focused on.' You get to the mountaintop and you look around, you're like 'oh god, what now?'"[216]

---

214 Lana Wilson, director, *Miss Americana*, Netflix Original Film, 2020.

215 Ibid.

216 Ibid.

Swift had to do a complete reset and understand why she was doing what she was doing and what was important to her. She needed to find her own happiness without the approval of others. She came to understand what her priorities were: her family and her friends.[217]

She had to deconstruct an entire belief system for her own personal sanity and happiness. Finally, while going through a reset, she reached a point where she was happy, and it wasn't in the way she was trained to be happy. She was happy without anyone else's input or opinion. When she found that, she decided to roll up her sleeves and get back to doing what she loved most: writing music and sharing her story.

She said, "After thirteen years of constantly feeling like I was misunderstood, knowing that everything that happened was all going to turn into this moment, you know, there's this thing people say about celebrities that they're frozen up in the age they got famous. And that's kind of what happened to me. I had a lot of growing up to do just trying to catch up to twenty-nine."[218]

In her diary from 2003, she found an entry that hit close to her heart:

"I tried to practice my song, but I completely psyched myself out and broke down crying. I don't know if I can do this. I want it so bad, but I get so scared of what might happen. I

---

217 Ibid.
218 Ibid.

can handle it. I'm young and talented; they'll see it in me. I've got to hang on."[219]

Her ability to reflect on every album and improve upon it is the reason why she's one of the biggest stars in music today. Swift's willingness to go over her most vulnerable moments has led her to the success she's found. Despite everything she's gone through, she doesn't want to change anything. In an interview with *PopSugar*, she said she wouldn't give her past self any advice. She would "have done everything exactly the same way. Because even the really tough things [she'd] gone through taught [her] things [she] never would have learned any other way."[220]

Swift appreciates her experience, even the ups and the downs. And today, she highlights how she wants to continue leading her career the way she started:

"I want to still have a sharp pen, a thin skin, and an open heart."[221]

Swift showcases what all creators need to do; we need to reflect, reconnect, and refocus. While you're working and achieving, it's easy to lose sight of your priorities. It seems counterintuitive, but if you look backwards often and reflect, you'll be one step ahead when you're moving forward. Understanding your priorities and initial goals are key to success in any creative endeavor.

---

219 Lana Wilson, director, *Miss Americana*, Netflix Original Film, 2020.

220 Kelsie Gibson, "Looking Back Now, Taylor Swift Wouldn't Give Her Younger Self Any Advice," *PopSugar*, December 13, 2019.

221 Lana Wilson, director, *Miss Americana*, Netflix Original Film, 2020.

SEEING HOW EVERYTHING CONNECTS

Along with realigning with your priorities, it's also important to understand how every moment along your journey connects. We need to adapt this mindset: every single experience in our life will bring us to another amazing journey.

Melanie Perkins, CEO and founder of Canva, the graphic design app that changed the world of creating for everyone, does this well. In 2020, she actually released a blog post reflecting on her experiences and explaining the importance of constant reflection to grow in your creativity.

She initially came up with the idea while in college in Perth, Australia. She couldn't understand why graphic designing tools were so difficult to use. They weren't user-friendly at all and cost an arm and a leg to get. She decided to start working on creating a new tool to help creators make it easy to create visuals. It wasn't always Canva though. Perkins first started by creating a platform and group to help schools design yearbooks more efficiently. They started small. They were able to get people to use their services in different places around the world, but it still wasn't the prettiest product. She regrouped and decided to go bigger: create a user-friendly platform for anyone to design online without downloading any fancy software.[222]

It wasn't too difficult to get users. After all, they had two strong pillars: there was a crowd that yearned for an easier way to design, and their company was built on the mantra that

222 Melanie Perkins, "21 Questions from Aussie Startups: Highs, Lows & Lessons learned during Canva's Journey So Far," *LinkedIn*, January 16, 2018.

everyone could create without friction. By 2020, Canva had over 15 million active users and 300,000 paying subscribers and they calculated that their users made 3,000 designs per minute.[223]

The main reason for Canva's success was their ability to reflect on *why* they created the platform. Their work makes peoples' lives easier. They target marketers, content creators, and students. Now, anyone can create a quality social media post, Facebook ad, blog post, or fancy PowerPoint. You can do all of that, and it isn't hard. That's the magic to a successful company. You need to reflect to keep up.

Steve Jobs is someone else who always drove this message home. At the end of his life, he talked about how we have to reflect on moments in our lives because sometimes certain moments lead up to others, and we'll see that they all connect.[224] Because you made one decision, another one will be able to connect, and you can trace that all the way back to your childhood, understanding how you ended up where you are today. I absolutely love stories like this. Listening to Steve Jobs explain this in his commencement speech was so impactful. It's true, you can tie back what you do today to what you did before.[225]

"You can't connect the dots looking forward; you can only connect them looking backwards. So, you have to trust that the dots will somehow connect in your future. You have to

---

223 Ibid.

224 *Stanford*, "Steve Jobs' 2005 Stanford Commencement Address," March 7, 2008, video, 15:04.

225 Ibid.

trust in something—your gut, destiny, life, karma, whatever. This approach has never let me down, and it has made all the difference in my life."[226]

It really is important to look backward and see how everything that you've done today connects because that might also be able to tell you what the future holds. Think about it this way: if you don't take the time to reflect and put in the work, you will repeat your mistakes. So, avoid the hassle in the future, and take the time to reflect now.

---

226 Yogi Putra, "What I Learned from Steve Jobs' Connecting The Dots," *Medium*, April 4, 2019.

PART 5

BECOMING A
MASTER CREATOR

14.

THINK CREATIVITY,
NOT PRODUCTIVITY

———

"There's a way to do it better—find it"

- THOMAS A. EDISON

pro·duc·tiv·i·ty
/ˌprōˌdəkˈtivədē, ˌprädəkˈtivədē/

noun

the effectiveness of productive effort, especially in industry, as measured in terms of the rate of output per unit of input.

ex. "workers have boosted productivity by 30 percent"[227]

---

227 Oxford Languages, Version 12.4., s.v. "Productivity," Oxford University Press, 2021.

We're in a world that's obsessed with productivity, and productivity is as old as America itself. There are podcasts, apps, programs, and journals dedicated to teaching us how to be more productive and enhance our workplace performance, which in turn "should" improve our lives. You'll find study after study looking at increased productivity in the workplace and how to improve work-life balance. We're often told to take a break to step away from our desks or work, but we're also reminded to make sure we're productive and working efficiently at all times. As workers, we're obsessed with getting things done.

According to Laura Vanderkam, author of *What the Most Successful People Do at Work*, "successful people know that hours, like capital, can be consciously allocated with the goal of creating riches—in the form of a changed world, life's work—overtime."[228]

Professor at Harvard College and author of *Stumbling on Happiness* Daniel Gilbert argues "a wandering mind is not a happy mind." Instead, we should schedule and manage our time wisely to reach full happiness.[229]

Cal Newport, author of *Deep Work* and the guy behind the Study Hacks Blog, noted that we need to schedule every single minute of every day. Create a list of things you need to do and assign a time period to do each task.[230]

---

228 Laura Vanderkam, *What the Most Successful People Do at Work: A Short Guide to Making Over Your Career* (New York: the Penguin Group, 2013), 1-60.

229 Daniel Gilbert, *Stumbling on Happiness* (New York: Alfred A. Knopf, 2007), 366.

230 Cal Newport, *Deep Work* (New York: Grand Central Publishing, 2016), 304.

Also, a study by Peter Gollwitzer, Psychology professor at NYU, states we need to stop fantasizing about our future successes and create a plan of action instead.[231]

These are all studies or pieces on how to enhance your productivity both in work and life, which in turn should lead us to a, quote-unquote, better life with more professional achievement and success. But are we really being successful simply by scheduling ourselves to capacity in an effort to make ourselves more productive? Shouldn't the idea of quality over quantity be the approach in any business putting out a product or any artist putting out work?

The problem is: *productivity is killing creativity.*

There's a clear tension between productivity and creativity. We're told we need to stop daydreaming, and instead, focus on the task at hand by setting goals every step of the way. We're shown how wealthy and "successful" people manage their time by spending it like money.

Today, we're taught that productivity leads to better performance or praise in the workplace, which results in better roles and ends with better pay and a "happier" life. As Michael Roberto, author of *Unlocking Creativity* writes, "Leaders and organizations claim to value creativity, but they often harbor biases and perpetuate environments to discourage new ideas."[232]

---

231 Peter Gollwitzer, *The Psychology of Action: Link Cognition and Motivation to Behavior* (New York: The Guilford Press, 1996), 683.

232 Michael Roberto, *Unlocking Creativity* (New Jersey: John Wiley & Sons, 2019), 208.

Instead, we turn to more measurable outcomes and processes like the rate of productivity. In 2014, Adobe found that 75 percent of employees said they were undergoing pressure to be productive rather than creative at work, and only half of Americans chose to describe themselves as creative (with the global average even lower at 39 percent).[233] Adobe marked this as the creative gap: the knowledge that creativity is key to success in any company, but the inability to tap into it. The issue is productive people complete items on checklists and work to accomplish task after task. Creative people are different; they need time to flow, disengage, and observe what already exists.

As we've noticed, creative work is not repetitive assembly work either. Creative workers are motivated by the work they're doing every day. They're motivated by their ability to make a difference. In a world where we're always preoccupied by media, work, family obligations, outings, status, and wealth, we rarely take a moment to do things unstimulated.

How do we become more creative? We gain more knowledge. Creativity is tied directly to the acquisition of knowledge and using it in different ways. Like Picasso and other artists, we need to take what we see in front of us and create something based off of our own vision. Many times, artists mimic other artists or things they see in the world to create their own masterpiece. We do the same with creating new ideas to solve the world's problems.

Take James Dyson for instance. He took something that was already invented and was able to improve it for another use.

---

233 Rupal Parekh, "Global Study: 75% Of People Think They're Not Living Up To Creative Potential," *AdAge,* April 23, 2012.

He was disappointed with his vacuum cleaner bag and wanted to find a way to make a better one. While visiting a local sawmill, he noticed how the sawdust was being removed from the air through the use of industrial cyclones. That's when the idea sparked. As an engineer, he got to work creating a smaller version. While it took him over five thousand tries to finally get it right, he was able to create a smaller scale cyclone and invented the first bagless vacuum cleaner.[234]

Instead of focusing on getting tasks one and two done on our to-do lists, we need to set time to achieve absolutely nothing. We need to start with just absorbing what's around us with no agenda or goal. In addition to acquiring more knowledge through having unstimulated time, we need to allow ourselves to fall into deep daydreams and take time to explore freely.

Sometimes the best ideas come to you when you're able to connect pieces together. Take it from composer and actor Lin-Manuel Miranda. Before creating *Hamilton*, the hit original Broadway production on Alexander Hamilton, Miranda was lounging in a hammock in Mexico reading Ron Chernow's 2004 biography *Alexander Hamilton*. That's when the idea hit him. He thought the story would present itself well as a musical. He started working on a mixtape called "The Hamilton Mixtape," which included a collection of hip-hop verses and melodies. It wasn't an overnight success. It took him seven years to write it and actually get it on the Broadway stage.[235]

---

234 Malone-Kircher, Madison, "James Dyson on 5,126 Vacuums That Didn't Work-and the One That Finally Did," *New York Magazine*, November 16, 2016.

235 Anna Almendrala, "Lin-Manuel Miranda It's 'No Accident' Hamilton Came To Me On Vacation," *Landit,* May 26, 2018.

According to Manoush Zomorodi, author of *Bored and Brilliant: How Spacing Out Can Unlock Your Most Productive and Creative Self,* reclaiming your time and creativity through moments of offline boredom is a long-term, empowering, and effective endeavor. Zomorodi conducted a study, recounted in her book. She drew thousands of participants and measured how they used their time. She wanted to see if people used their time better if they were away from their phones and other devices. Prior to the study, participants reported using their phone for an average of two hours a day, picking them up sixty times daily. She had various experiments challenge their habits. First, she asked participants to pocket their phone for one day and avoid checking the screen. During the challenge, participants had strong urges to take their phone out of their pocket. When they didn't check their phone, she saw an immediate boost in creativity. The next study, they had to delete their favorite app for at least one day. After deleting their favorite app, the participants shared that they felt emotions like sadness and loneliness. At the same time, though, they felt less guilty about wasting their time on their phones. In her book, Zomorodi notes that behavioral change takes time. And by the end of the week of challenges, participants had reduced their phone use to an average of only six minutes per day.[236]

Zomorodi found that people can be their most creative selves when they are able to detach and process the world around them.

---

236 Manoush Zomorodi, *Bored and Brilliant: How Spacing Out Can Unlock Your Most Productive and Creative Self* (New York: St. Martin's Press, 2017), 208.

We need to start creating time and space for people to explore. Take Google, one of the most innovative companies in the world, for example. They maintain their competitive and innovative edge because Google encourages its employees to devote 20 percent of their time to side projects. When companies allow their employees to invest time into other outlets that they're excited about, they end up with amazing new products that started off as side projects: Gmail, Google Maps, Twitter, Slack, Groupon, and more.[237]

So, instead of focusing on your goals and lists, take time to focus on nothing and just let your mind wander. Set some time in your week to do so. The more space you give yourself to achieve absolutely nothing and absorb the world around you, the more opportunity you'll have to connect what you see so you can create your own art. Successful entrepreneurs know how important it is to take a step back and allow themselves the chance to stop worrying about productivity and focus on creativity.

Like Thomas A. Edison said, "there's a way to do it better—find it."[238] But to add to that, I believe there *is* a way to do it better, but don't find it; flow with it and see where your creative imagination takes you.

237 Adam Robinson, "Want to Boost Your Bottom Line? Encourage Your Employees to Work on Side Projects," *Inc*, March 12, 2018.

238 Dan Scalco, "23 Powerful Quotes to Get Your Creativity Flowing," *Inc*, January 23, 2018.

15.

IF YOU DON'T KNOW, HAVE A GO

———

It was 8:39 on Friday morning, and I was just starting to get settled down in chemistry when Dr. Silverman posed a difficult question to the entire class. I immediately realized that I did not know the answer to the question, and my knee-jerk reaction was to quickly look down at my notebook in order to avoid eye contact. I panicked at the thought of Dr. Silverman calling my name and forcing me to admit stupidity in front of the entire class that I had no answer.

Despite my attempts to shield myself from her gaze, Dr. Silverman called my name. My face turned bright red, and it was obvious that I didn't know the answer to the question. There were two possible ways that I could handle this situation. Number one: I could admit that I did not know the answer, or number two: I could attempt to answer and possibly get the problem wrong in front of the entire class. Either way I had to face the embarrassment that followed.

Have you ever experienced this? Which option would you choose? Rather than attempting to solve the problem outright, we often languish in our fear of being wrong and making mistakes. Why are we so afraid of being wrong? Why are we frightened of making mistakes?

In any creative endeavor, you'll face moments like this. So, it's important to know how and why we react the way we do in these situations.

First off, what is fear?

According to the website *How Stuff Works*, the scientific definition of fear is "a chain reaction in the brain that starts with a stressful stimulus and ends with the release of chemicals that cause a racing heart, fast breathing and energized muscles, also known as the fight-or-flight response."[239] This stimulus could be as simple as sitting in class, afraid of giving the wrong answer, or even presenting a speech in front of a large group of people. For some reason, we humans are afraid of admitting our lack of knowledge by being wrong. We have a perception that mistakes equate to embarrassment. As such, rather than attempting to solve a problem, we hide in fear of making mistakes and embarrassing ourselves.

This all ties back to how we view successful and smart people. There's a myth that smart people are never wrong and never make mistakes but, actually, no matter how smart the individual is, they will still make errors. According to *Forbes*

---

239 Craig Freudenrich and Robynne Boyd, "How Your Brain Works," *HowStuffWorks*, June 25, 2020.

magazine, the difference is that "smart people don't fear being wrong because they know that being wrong is ultimately an instrument that pushes them closer to being right."[240] The main lesson here is that being wrong does not mean you are unintelligent. In fact, being wrong teaches you what is right. Sure, making a mistake by being wrong in front of all your peers can be mortifying, but at least you tried. We can't always live in fear of making mistakes and being embarrassed.

Remember the days when we used to play with blocks and fight over being the line leader? Well, young children tend to learn more than adults because they are neither scared of embarrassment nor scared of making mistakes. Kenneth Robinson, an educationalist, explained in his well-known TED Talk, "Kids will take a chance. If they don't know, they'll have a go. They're not frightened of being wrong." I observed this in my early childhood development class. The preschoolers were not afraid of experimenting and expressing their ideas. One Wednesday, a preschooler named Diya tapped me on my back and asked, "Can you read this to me?" It took me a while to figure out what she was talking about.

She walked me to the art station and pointed to her drawing. My first reaction was to question what Diya was trying to show. On the piece of paper, there were scribbled lines which appeared to be letters in a random order. I read the paper out loud, "sin-dre-lla." I repeated the word in my head until finally Diya smiled and said, "Yeah! Cinderella." For us, Cinderella may not be a complicated word, but for a four-year-old, she

---

240 Alice Walton, "7 Assumptions Smart People Never Make," *Forbes*, January 24, 2014.

attempted to sound out and spell a four-syllable word that consists of ten letters. Despite her not knowing how to spell Cinderella, Diya made an attempt without the fear of being wrong. In fact, she was very proud of her accomplishment. She was not afraid of making a mistake.

As we become older, we become more conscious about others around us and about how awkward situations can be created because of our actions. We are trained to fear making mistakes and being wrong. In elementary school, the students who had the correct answers were always rewarded with the gold stars. As a book critic from the *New York* magazine explains, those who were incorrect were considered to be "the dumb kid, the troublemaker, the one who never does homework. So, by the time you are nine years old, you've already learned that people who get stuff wrong are lazy, irresponsible dimwits."[241] To this day, we always strive for the gold star without thinking about the hidden gems behind learning from mistakes. Rather than facing the challenge, we are scared of being wrong, and as a result we literally hide from the teacher when we do not know the correct answer. We need to realize that making mistakes by being wrong is part of the journey to earning the gold star.

In life, we will always be faced with situations similar to chemistry class, and there is no way of avoiding that. As I continue to grow older, I am more aware of the fact that I know very little. It's okay to not know everything and it's okay to be wrong. In fact, it's okay to make mistakes, as long

---

241 Michael Roberto, *Creative Confidence: Unleashing the Creative Potential Within Us All* (New York: Crown Publishing, 2013), 304.

as you ask for help and learn from them. When you face something that you are unsure of, do not sit and hide; face the challenge head on. What is the worst that can happen? I will make a mistake and inevitably learn something. The worst thing that could happen is that you make a mistake, from which you can then learn something rather than seeing it as a failed venture. Best case scenario, you succeed and realize you were capable of something you hadn't even realized. My high school chemistry class often reminds me that I'm not always going to be correct, and I am continually reminded that I should not be apprehensive to admit this to myself and those around me.

Take entrepreneur, politician, and author Stacey Abrams for example. You may also know her as former Georgia gubernatorial candidate who then turned voting rights advocate and worked to turn Georgia blue for Joe Biden. Outside of politics, Abrams is an incredible entrepreneur.

Abrams has faced many setbacks through her life. When she told an interviewer that her goal was to become president one day, she recalled that "[she] faced screams of, 'How dare [she] speak aloud such a dramatic ambition?'"[242] But, you need to realize the minute we allow ourselves to be silenced or be told we can't achieve is the moment we begin to weaken who we are and what we're capable of.

As Abrams so aptly put it, "The goal should always be to challenge yourself and explore your potential—even when

242 Jessica Stillman, "Stacey Abrams Has 5 Powerful Words for Anyone Who Thinks They Aren't Cut Out for Success," *Inc*, January 6, 2021.

you know you will not necessarily be first or the best. I advise people to be aware of their own fear because that fear can sometimes be masking your ambition. Getting over that fear can unleash your drive and potential—leading you down a path of prosperity that probably would not have been obtainable had you not taken the first step out of your comfort zone."[243]

Remember: "Fear is a common obstacle that impacts everyone. It eats away at the confidence, ambition, and dreams of individuals who cannot imagine themselves in certain spaces. We are also often influenced by stories of individuals who took bold, courageous steps but also sacrificed a lot in the process or didn't succeed. We must remember that being bold and courageous is bigger than just us, our feelings, and our successes. Those who depend on us to improve their lives can give us the courage we need to take chances and help us find bravery we might not have had otherwise. You should never say no for yourself. Others will do that for you."[244]

Do not be afraid of admitting to yourself, and those around you, that you are wrong. And never allow yourself to edit your own ambition because of your fear. Being wrong helps lead you down a more creative path and opens up your possibilities. If you're always conscious of what you're doing wrong, you'll never reach your full potential. The fear of being wrong can easily be conquered when you take the first step and accept that it is okay to make errors. It seems that we should not just aspire to be right, but rather focus on learning from our

---

243 Ibid.

244 Ibid.

mistakes. We should not avoid the unknown because of our fear. Next time you face a challenging obstacle remember one thing, there is nothing wrong with being wrong.

Here are a few ways you can overcome the fear of failure and being wrong:

1. Go by the *abundance mentality*, meaning the mindset that there is plenty out there for everyone.

2. Practice doing things outside of your comfort zone.

3. The most intelligent people actually try to be wrong on purpose. Everything requires trial and error.

4. Remember, you learn more from being wrong.

5. And remember that everyone is wrong sometimes!

As Tom and David Kelley, professors at Stanford and authors of *Creative Confidence*, explain, it's important to nurture our creative confidence. Creativity is a muscle we need to exercise often. When you act on your own ideas, you realize the power of your own creative strengths. And to nurture that muscle, we need to understand that being wrong is okay. We need to dare to go from fear to courage.[245]

Psychologist Albert Bandura discovered the liberating effect of using "guided mastery" to get over being afraid of our

---

245 Michael Roberto, *Creative Confidence: Unleashing the Creative Potential Within Us All* (New York: Crown Publishing, 2013), 304.

skills and work. Bandura explains that this method requires a sequence of challenges to help us eliminate our fears. Every time you face a more difficult challenge, you persevere and become more resilient. According to Bandura, that mix of resilience and persistence is "self-efficacy." We need to continue to challenge ourselves and put ourselves in difficult situations to enhance our creative selves and understand our full potential.[246]

Think about it this way: eleven out of twelve businesses fail.[247]

Yes. That's right.

Eleven of twelve. So, that means only one in twelve businesses actually succeed. But if people didn't take a risk because they were scared of being wrong, we wouldn't have the technology and innovation that we have today. Imagine if Steve Jobs decided not to take a risk and create the Apple I. What if Airbnb gave up on improving the world of hospitality and travel? Where would we be if Vinton Cerf and Bob Kahn stopped working on creating the internet?

Failure and setbacks are inevitable, but it's your responsibility to keep going.

Will you reach every ambitious goal you set for yourself?

---

246 Albert Bandura, Edward Blanchard and Brunhilde Ritter, "Relative Efficacy of Desensitization and Modeling Approaches For Inducing Behavioral, Affective, and Attitudinal Changes," *Journal of Personality and Social Psychology* 13, no. 6 (1969): 173-199.

247 Sean Bryant, "How Many Startups Fail and Why?," *Investopedia*, November 9, 2020.

Probably not.

Will you experience failure and setbacks?

Of course.

But everything will work itself out, and it's worth it to try.

Because sometimes failures help us arrive where we need to be. Jonah Lehrer, author of *Imagine: How Creativity Works*, explains, "Before we can find the answer—before we can even know the question—we must be immersed in disappointment, convinced that a solution is beyond our reach. We need to have wrestled with the problem and lost. Because it's only after we stop searching that an answer may arrive."[248]

So, don't be afraid to face challenges and be wrong no matter the situation. You get up, learn from it, and find your most creative self in the process.

---

248 Maria Popova, "The Importance of Frustration in the Creative Process Animated," *Brain Pickings*, November 2, 2015.

16.

WHY NOW?

———

C reativity starts when kids are three to five years old. Their world is full of imagination, magic, and has no bounds. Scholastic found that "for many, their creativity will reach its peak before the age of six, after which it will begin to decline with the onset of formal schooling and the developmental drive towards conformity."[249] I've seen this firsthand with my younger brother.

One day, when my brother was in kindergarten, he came running down the stairs to pack a few of his toys in his back-pack before school. While preparing breakfast, my mom took notice of his packing, and she gave my dad "the look" to check up on him. My dad walked over to my brother and told him, "Aaron, you can only bring one toy to school." Aaron looked disappointed; he wanted to show his friends all of his new Thomas the Tank Engine trains, which were very cool at the time. He then went on to somberly remove all of the toy trains from his bag.

---

249 Michelle Anthony, "Creative Development in 3-5 Year Olds" *Scholastic,* 2020.

We all returned to our normal breakfast routine, until we heard a *click, click, click.* We turned around and looked at my brother. He was magnetically connecting twelve of his favorite trains—Thomas, Gordon, Percy, James, Edward, and so on.

We all looked at him with disbelief. My dad bent over to talk to him again, "Aaron, I said only one toy." My five-year-old brother looked up at my dad and said, "Yeah, it's one!"

My mom and I started laughing from the breakfast table. My little brother was so creative and there was no denying it. To this day, I marvel at the level of pure creativity—and possible rebellion—my then five-year-old brother had. Even at thirteen, I would not have thought in such an outside the box way, because I had already begun conforming to the creative standards of society for my age.

For years, I looked back at this story. He was so creative coming up with solutions to problems he was facing in the world. And that's when I noticed we rarely reward creativity, especially as kids grow up.

Instead, we're taught to *follow the plan.* At twenty-one, I still don't know what that plan consists of or why it's the *recipe for success.* We live in a world that discourages mistakes, risk-taking and exploration, especially for kids. We're raised to fear failure and shame. According to *Psychology Today,* "People who have a fear of failure are motivated to avoid failing not because they cannot manage the basic emotions of disappointment, anger, and frustration that accompany such experiences but because failing *also* makes them feel deep shame."[250] As a society, we shield children from issues to protect them. Instead, we're adding to a self-conscious, fear-based existence that chips away the walls of curiosity and therefore creativity. Even in workplaces, leaders sacrifice the opportunities that lie within creativity in order to stay productive and efficient.

As kids, we have a natural curiosity for the world around us, and we need to find a way to tap into that and bring out the creative-no-bounds-kid in all of us.

But how exactly do we do that? First, we need to figure out our own personal strengths to understand how to unlock our creativity. Teacher, historian, and author Lynne Levesque studied the importance of completing tests like Myers-Briggs to figure out our best abilities.[251]

Every combination of letters has a different meaning and skillset. For example, if you're an ESTP—Extraverted, Observant, Thinking, and Prospecting—you're an entrepreneur, which means you are a practical person who is open to the world. Entrepreneurs learn through experience and get impatient when they feel like nothing is happening. ESTPs are always on their feet looking for ways to explore. If you're an INFJ—Introverted, Intuitive, Feeling, and Judging—on the other hand, like I am, you're an Advocate. Advocates lead life with a thoughtful and imaginative approach. They take

250 Guy Winch, "10 Signs That You Might Have Fear Of Failure," *Psychology Today*, June 18, 2013.

251 Lynne Leveque, *Breakthrough Creativity: Achieving Top Performance Using the Eight Creative Talents* (Kansas City: Nicholas Brealey, 2011), 228.

concrete steps to achieve their goals and make an impact in the world, and they're known for their passion, creativity, and imagination.

I'd definitely take the test, if you haven't already, to figure out what your personality type is. Once you understand how you function and best operate, you can start breaking down your barriers and become your most creative and innovative self. Our problem is we often think that only one type of personality is creative when actually, it's clear that everyone has different traits or techniques that make them uniquely creative. Remember, creativity is very different from knowledge. Often, we think creativity and knowledge are one in the same. Instead, we need to focus on how creativity is more about analyzing and connecting ideas to come up with new, innovative solutions.

Understanding how we function and how to be more creative is crucial and isn't just important to us individually, it's key to the entire human existence. Without creativity, we wouldn't be where we are today. In the early 2000s, companies like Adobe and IBM did research on the importance of creativity in the workplace. In 2012, Adobe's study found that eight in ten felt that unlocking creativity was critical to economic growth but only one in four believed they were living up to their own creative potential.[252]

In 2010, IBM conducted a similar study on creativity being the most crucial factor for success.[253] The study highlighted

252 "IBM 2010 Global CEO Study: Creativity Selected as Most Crucial Factor for Future Success," IBM, May 18, 2010.

253 *"IBM 2010 Global CEO Study: Creativity Selected as Most Crucial Factor for Future Success,"* IBM, May 18, 2010.

the importance of creative leaders and CEOs. Creativity was shown to help in problem solving during complex situations and led to better performance for all groups and roles. So now we know that creativity is important to our work. In fact, some of the biggest companies have emphasized that. But how come we're still stuck valuing other traits over creativity? It would seem it's because we don't believe that we can learn how to become creative.

Creativity isn't a skill you're given, it's something that can be developed. There's an opportunity for everyone to be able to tap into that creative mindset and be curious like a kid. How do we get there? Creativity really starts with knowledge. As my inner INFJ says, we have to take a thoughtful and imaginative approach and lead everything we do with passion, creativity, and imagination.

Creativity requires analyzing, thinking, processing, and connecting. It's also not easy, but you've got it.

It's important to keep studying the ever-changing and evolving art of creativity, as it helps us move forward in innovating and solving problems. Today, society is not set up to encourage creativity. In *The Rise of the Creative Class*, author Richard Florida argues there's a new class in our midst: the Creative Class, a group of people who aim to improve our work by conquering their skill and improving the world.[254] In order to make the change we desire in the world, we need to take a creative approach to solve challenges along the way. We need

254 Richard Florida, *The Rise of the Creative Class: And How It's Transforming Work, Leisure, Community, and Everyday Life* (New York: Brilliance Audio 2014), 404.

to understand what is inhibiting our creative imagination and how we can push past it to put together solutions to the world's complex and unique challenges ahead.

Ken Robinson, author of *Out of Our Minds*, argues that one way to move forward is to improve our school system.[255] Schools stand in the way of our creative imagination and we need to challenge and completely renovate the education systems that exist now.

While it sounds good to change the school system, we need to realize that optimizing creative learning is a systemic change. It definitely won't happen overnight. Take my mom for example. When looking for preschools for my little brother, she wanted to make sure he was prepared to join the "big kids" in elementary school. She came across this one pre-school: Little Red Wagon. They took pride in their curriculum. Instead of focusing on having every child meet certain educational requirements, they made sure each student had the opportunity to do what they had fun doing. So, when my three-year-old brother decided to go over and play with the blocks, they didn't prevent him from doing it even though all the other kids were learning the alphabet song. This was a hard concept for my mom to swallow. Her initial thought was that he wouldn't be learning and wasn't meeting the goals and requirements. She later realized, though, that this approach proved effective. Today, my brother is extremely creative in how he views the world and makes decisions. While "changing the school system" to focus more on free-flowing passion and

255 Ken Robinson, *Out of Our Minds: Learning to be Creative* (Westford, MA: Capstone, 2011), 352.

creativity is nice to say, it's hard to make happen, especially as we're so used to rules, guidelines, and expectations.

But changing the way we exist today is crucial to our survival because "the more complex the world becomes, the more creative we need to be to meet its challenges."[256]

So, remember that creativity isn't a trait that belongs solely to artists. Instead of focusing on how only a few are "creatives," we need to understand that everyone can be creative no matter what they pursue. We need to tap into our natural curiosity and interest to explore. We need to look directly at our ability to look at the world around us and observe what needs correcting and how we can go about fixing it. We won't bring about real change in the world until we're all able to be creative freely.

The question isn't "Why now?" The question is "Why is our society still behind?"

We're in a world that favors productivity and preserving somewhat-successful ideas far more than creativity and embracing wholly new ways of solving problems, and we need to change that. Instead of focusing on the "what," we need to hone in on the "how." If we figure out how creative people were able to start the companies that exist today, compose music, produce TV and movies, and create works of art, then we can better highlight the importance of how they did it and give less emphasis on what they did and how much they accomplished.

---

256 Ibid.

17.

YOU'RE MORE CREATIVE THAN YOU THINK

———

I f you had told me four years ago that I would one day be a published author, I probably would have laughed. Even a few months before I started writing this book, I giggled at the idea.

I was in the Target parking lot with my used-to-be-babysitter and now close friend Olivia, and I vividly remember walking in the half-empty, lamp-lit lot before closing. At the time, I was going through a rough patch, a mid-life-crisis-that-actually-took-place-at-twenty, you could say. I didn't know what my next move was. All I knew was I felt incomplete. While going through this transitional phase, I asked Olivia a question that I assumed there was no answer for:

"What now? Things haven't been going as planned. What should I do?"

Olivia replied with what seemed like a joke at the time, "You should write a book!"

Looking back, I remember we both laughed it off. It seemed like such a nonsensical answer to the question because I couldn't imagine myself writing and publishing a book.

Crazily enough, this moment and many other decisions I made tie back to my fourth-grade self. Not only had I left my dream of becoming a young adult novelist behind when I hid my notebook in the back of my closet, but I lost a part of me that believed in my own creativity.

When you think about yourself, would you say you're creative? Most people, when asked, would probably say "no."

I hope, however, that after reading this book you have a greater understanding of creativity and yourself. Creativity is inherent in all of us. Sometimes it just takes some practice and effort to pull it out and utilize it. By following the lessons in this book and listening to the stories of other creatives, you may find that being creative is a lot easier to do than you thought and perhaps pursuing that idea you have isn't really so daunting after all. The biggest thing that holds most people back is the idea that they aren't and don't know how to be creative. So, we have to figure out how to really unlock that creative mindset to succeed at every level, whether you're a student, already in business, or you're thinking of pursuing your own venture.

TL;DR

As you go through your own creative endeavor, I hope you keep these lessons in mind:

LEAD WITH AN ENTREPRENEURIAL MINDSET.

Think of entrepreneurship as the pursuit of problem-solving, innovation, and creative thinking. You don't necessarily have to start your own business to be an entrepreneur, but there are key aspects in every entrepreneur and creator that are crucial in each endeavor.

YOU DON'T HAVE TO BE A GENIUS.

So often, we look at creative people as geniuses. We don't believe that we can be creative too. No matter what people say, you don't have to be a genius to do great things. We have to demystify the idea that one has to be a Mark Zuckerberg or Taylor Swift and embrace that we, too, can succeed in a creative venture. Creativity shouldn't be a competition. It should be an opportunity for exploration and growth.

BE DISRUPTIVE.

Disruptive creators are unwilling to settle, often follow the road less traveled, and make a place for themselves through their work. While it can be scary to go out of a limb, the most successful creative people embrace uncertainty and the unknown. While the path leads to hurdles and difficulty, it will also lead to more significant insights, experience, and knowledge.

YOU CAN MANIPULATE YOUR MOTIVATION.
Once you understand what excites you and what drives you, you'll have the ability to uncover and manipulate your own motivation. We need to reflect and rediscover what excites us. Looking back, why did you start doing something? What drew you to it in the first place? Where are you now? Once you understand your journey, you'll understand more about the root of your passion and purpose. And once you rediscover your passion, you'll have the fuel you need to keep going.

THERE'S POWER IN PERSEVERANCE.
The truth is the creative journey won't be full of rainbows and butterflies. It'll be hard sometimes, and you have to be the one who figures out how much difficulty you're willing to take. Sometimes, you need to take on two jobs to pursue your creative passion project and earn money to pay the bills. Other times, you need to find a way to better manage your work-life balance. At all times, you need to figure out what your priorities are. Make sure you're doing what works best for you and be good at gauging what is worth it.

EMBRACE AUTHENTICITY, EVEN IF IT'S SCARY.
Listen to your heart and pour it into your work. Like many self-starters and passionate people do, pour everything you have into what you love. The worst that can happen is you figure out it wasn't for you and need to redirect. Don't miss an opportunity because you didn't want to put your whole self into it. Being authentic only elevates your creative endeavors, as it builds your identity, gives substance to what you're

offering, and enables people to relate and engage with you. While it can be daunting, it's worth the risk.

YOU CAN CREATE YOUR OWN LUCK.

At the end of the day, spotting an "amazing idea" or business opportunity won't happen in the spur of the moment. It takes preparation, pure interest, and dedication. Creative people notice opportunities, choose to pursue them by listening to their gut, stay positive, and adopt a resilient attitude. So, yes, you can create your own luck with the right attitude.

YOU'LL GO FURTHER TOGETHER.

As the African proverb says, "If you want to go fast, go alone. If you want to go far, go together." We've heard it time and time again; having a strong team is crucial to success in any endeavor. Building a great team doesn't mean you need the most brilliant people in a room together; you just need people who are interested in achieving the same goals. With driven and dedicated people from an array of experiences, we can achieve amazing results. Not to mention, creative collaboration happens over generations. Something created in the past can inspire something in the present, and something created in the present can impact the future. Creators have the ability to challenge generational innovation.

WHAT WOULD AN ENTERTAINER DO?

Traditionally, we see entertainers as performers and artists, but entertainers have many traits in common with entrepreneurs. Good entertainers, like entrepreneurs, are skilled in four areas: they're enthusiastic, confident, adaptable, and creative. Entrepreneurs can learn a lot from entertainers, from the art of storytelling to embracing a kid-like attitude. In fact, we should always ask ourselves *what would an entertainer do?*

BE PATIENT.

The best creators understand that creating and problem solving won't happen overnight, and they know it will take a lot of work and learning. Patience is an underrated force of creativity, and the best creators are patient with the work that they're doing.

IF THEY CAN DO IT, YOU CAN TOO!

Forget everyone in the world exists, and just be you. A lot of the time, we're self-conscious or lose belief in ourselves because we're worried about what other people will think or say. Instead of focusing on others, we need to trust our gut and believe that we know what we're doing, and we can do whatever we set our mind to. We've all heard the saying, "If you don't believe in yourself, no one else will." It's imperative in mastering creativity because if you don't think you're going to succeed, how will anyone else believe you will? Think about it, all the companies that exist right now were created by someone, so why can't that someone be you?

ALWAYS REFLECT SO YOU DON'T REPEAT.

Being a creative person requires a lot of self-reflection and self-understanding. You need to understand how you function to perform your most creatively. So, always reflect on how you got started, if your work follows your initial mission and vision, and how that can direct your future. If you reflect, you won't repeat the same mishaps.

THINK CREATIVITY, NOT PRODUCTIVITY.

We're often told to take a break to step away from our desks or work but also reminded to make sure we're productive and working efficiently at all times. As workers, we're obsessed with getting things done. So, instead of focusing on your goals and lists, take time to focus on nothing, and just let your mind wander. The more space you give yourself to achieve absolutely nothing and absorb the world around you, the more opportunity you'll have to connect what you see so you can create your own art. Successful entrepreneurs know how important it is to take a step back and allow themselves the chance to stop worrying about productivity and focus on creativity.

IF YOU DON'T KNOW, HAVE A GO.

Don't be afraid to face challenges and be wrong no matter the situation. You get up, learn from it, and find your most creative self in the process.

YOU GOT THIS! YOU'RE MORE CREATIVE THAN YOU THINK.

So, don't leave your composition notebook at the back of your closet. Embrace your creative ability because creativity will help you get where you want to be.

Abraham Lincoln once said,

*"The best way to predict the
future is to create it."*

Thanks for reading my creative endeavor; now go create yours!

AUTHOR'S NOTE

"The future isn't a place that we're going to go. It's a place that you get to create."

— NANCY DUARTE

I've always been a creator and artist, and baking is just one of my many artistic passions. You'll find me in the kitchen making cookies, breads, macaroons, fruit tarts, pastries, and more during my free time. My love for baking and creating led me to work at a bakery during my first gap year. I had a fantastic opportunity to learn more about baking at a professional cupcakery and also helped a local business grow in customers, sales, and social media presence through new and innovative ideas. That's when I found that my love for creating could lead to a profession in entrepreneurship.

Often, we have a stigma attached to pursuing creativity or art, but in my mind, entrepreneurship has always been a form of art. In fact, I believe my love for creating and artistry helped jump start my passion for social entrepreneurship.

Over the summer during my second gap year, I decided to pursue something I had always wanted to do: write a book. I sat down in my room, by the beach, or on the couch and wrote over forty-thousand words. This experience in and of itself has been so rewarding and eye-opening in exploring my own passion for entrepreneurship, and after completing the manuscript, I was excited to find publisher New Degree Press actually interested in sharing my book with the rest of the world. After painstakingly editing and iterating on my book, *Creative @ Work* officially hit bookstores!

As my second gap year continued, I wanted to find more opportunities to create solutions to today's problems. I collaborated with seasoned executives on media-tech startups, worked on app prototypes, pitched new ideas to VCs, and even found myself able to help founders from more than one hundred and six countries through work with Startup Grind, the world's largest community of startups, founders, innovators, and creators.

All of these experiences lead to my greatest aspiration: becoming a social entrepreneur post-college.

I'm inspired to write this book because I hope to find key traits that allow someone to come up with creative solutions to problems and find a way to effectively execute. So often, we look at business as a rigid, by-the-books field instead of a free-flowing, artistic, and creative endeavor. I've always seen the process of coming up with ideas as art. Being a young entrepreneur, I've always sought out this information in articles, videos, and interviews. I thought this book would create a way for me to:

- Learn more about a topic in which I've always been interested

- Be able to create a resource for others to learn about this topic

- Have a way to reflect on what I've learned and observed

The future is something we create, which is why I'm so drawn to writing about when our creativity is at work.

I hope you enjoy reading this work!

ACKNOWLEDGMENTS

———

Let me just start by saying, if you read all the way through this book to the end and have landed on this page, you should be acknowledged. Thank you for taking the time to read and support my work.

Behind every creative endeavor, there's a team. It's been quite a journey writing this book, and I'm so grateful for everyone who supported me along the way. My biggest accomplishment through this process was committing the time and energy to complete and edit this manuscript. I spent hours hunched over at my desk typing away until 5 a.m., cried over my inability to put my thoughts on paper, and persevered through the ever-stressful pre-sale and revisions process.

To all of my friends and family who encouraged my writing process, edited my words, and allowed me to vent about my frustrations, I am forever grateful.

Mom, Dad, Adrienne, and Aaron, thank you for putting up with me. I know none of you were expecting me to take another gap year mid-way through college, and I'm eternally grateful that you supported my decisions and ambition. You had a front-row seat to my procrastination, crying fits, and rewrites.

Grandma and Grandpa, thank you for helping me pre-sell my book! While I was under a fog of stress, you both helped me when I needed it by reaching out to our community and spreading the news. I really appreciate it and will never forget it.

Tita Sheila and Tito Ron, thank you for always believing in me. You've both been such a huge inspiration in my life and have always pushed me to dream bigger and work harder. Thank you for having me over to refresh and reset whenever I fall and reminding me of everything I have to offer.

Tita Suzzette, thank you so much for supporting me before I even completed my manuscript. Your words still ring in my ears. "I want to invest in you." Thank you for reminding me how much strong women can accomplish. Thank you for investing in me.

Olivia Smith, you saw this acknowledgment coming. In fact, I vividly remember you reminding me to acknowledge you in my book before I even thought about writing one. Thank you for encouraging me to write my first book! Growing up, you always shared your favorite books with me, engaged in insightful conversations on what we were reading, and believed in me when I didn't. Thank you! This book is a result of our late-night walk in the Target parking lot, which is crazy to look back upon. That night, I was struggling to figure out what my next steps would be. I asked you a question no one could really answer, "What now? Things haven't been going as planned, what should I do?" You replied with a joke, "You should write a book!" We both laughed it off and you added "And when you write it, add me in the acknowledgments and say I inspired it." Olivia, you most definitely did inspire it, and I am so grateful.

Adie Sprague, thank you from the bottom of my heart for showing me that someone's passion can become a business. I came to Treat thinking I'd pick up some baking tips and also surround myself with delicious cupcakes. I came away with far more. Thank you for believing in me and allowing me to step up in the café. Treat has taught me so much about work ethic, building a strong community, and creating for the love of making others happy. I hope to use the enthusiasm and creativity you put into everything you do into every aspect of my life.

To the team at New Degree Press, thank you for providing a platform to bring my book to life. Eric Koester, Brian Bies, Anne Kelley, and Michelle Pollack deserve special thanks.

This book was made possible because of a community of people who believed in me so fervently. They pre-ordered copies, helped me promote the book, and helped edit my manuscript. You are all amazing! Thank *you*.

Aaron Jung

Adam Marcelo

Adriana McNulty

Aileen Barbiellini Amidei & Bernardo Barbiellini

Alex Ewing

Alexa Lebron-Cruz

Alice Abaca

Aline McIntyre

Amber Yang

Amelia & Dario Lirio

Amy Wasserman

Ana Janina Pioquid

Anamaria Ferrer

Andrea Tang

Ann Pecho

Anna Maria Barbiellini

Anna Salas

Anne Pinto

Ariel Kohane

Asuncion Burgos

Ben Silvian

Benedict Acunin

Candy Francisco

Carina Vargad

Carlito Perez

Cattleya Musni

Cattleya Nery

Cecilia Lirio

Charlie Capalad

Chaya Ray

Chloe Mitchell & Ryan
Marcelo

Clare Perez

Clinton K Pong

Dan Dangler

David & Margarita Zarraga

David LaLiberte

David Lane

Dayan Abeyaratne

Dimitri Yang

Dylan Frassica

Ebbie Latunio

Eco Capalad

Eleanor Reyes

Elicie Edmond

Elisabeth Marchini

Elizabeth Ona Sweet

Erica & Sophia Scheik

Eufie Aburizeck

Ferdinand De Gala

Florina Pioquid

Gabrielle Corbin

Grace & Dante Perez

Grace & Dario Lirio

Graciela Price

Gregory Prado

Hannah Brukardt

Hermie Amolat

Hershey Roxas

Husnal Bhasin

Ifelia De Leon

Iris Nussbaum

Jack Shaw

Jaclyn Lo

Jaime Salama

Jane & Ricky Perez

Jayne Jocson

Jocelyn Capalad

Jocelyn Suarez

John Landy

John Reagan D Mendoza

Jose Perez

Joshua Bean

Julie Calderon

Jun Acunin

June & Dan Benedetti

Justin Cheong

Kateri Lirio

Katie Manyin

Kayla & Myrtha Chang

Kiana Lee

Kiana Moattari

Kim Ariyabuddhiphongs

Kimberly Flores

Kristine Lirio

Lauren Ragin

Lee Ortenberg

Leonisa Averion

Leticia Wark

Leticia Wark

Li Chen

Lorceli Sagullo

Madeleine Capino

Maggie Chan-Yu

Marah Capalad

Maria Batilo

Maria Jacob

Maria Minda Sagullo

Marilou Sagullo

Matt Brown

Megan Petero

Melba Consogno

Melizza Pacia

Meriwether Florence

Merly Dee

Michael Badaoui

Midori Sangiolo

Miguel Zialcita

Mona Baloch

Nathan Mark

Neil Patel

Nicholas Zhang

Nicole Lirio

Nilo Punzalan

Olivia Smith

Pauline Roxas

Phoebe Morales

Rachel Navarrette

Ramon Sagullo

Raquel Sagullo

Raul & Grace Lirio

Rebecca Patenia

Reiner See

Robert Paulino

Robert Sytangco

Rogelio Naranja

Rong & Jen Chen

Rosenaldo Maliwanag

Rosie Capalad

Roy & Shannon Lirio

Ruma Bose

Sheila & Ron Marcelo

Shivanthi Gunasekera

Soledad Banea

Sophie Shimazu

Stan Zheng

Steph Nussbaum

Suzie Na

Suzzette Ona

Theresa Tabib

Tommy Jankowski

Tita Monica & Tito Gadi Laredo

Tony Yip

Tricie Ledakis

Trish Stevenson

Trishia Lichauco

Victor, Cathy, Sarah & Becca Ona

Vir Montecillo

Vivian & Steve Wolfson

William Huang

Zaynab Ghazi

APPENDIX

INTRODUCTION

Bosma, Niels and Donna Kelley. "Global Entrepreneurship Monitor." *Impactful Entrepreneurship* 20, no. 2.3 (2018): 26-27. https://www.babson.edu/media/babson/site-assets/content-assets/academics/centers-and-institutes/the-arthur-m-blank-center-for-entrepreneurship/global-research/gem-2018-2019-global-report.pdf.

Duffin, Erin. "Number of Bachelor's Degrees Earned in the United States in 2017/18." https://www.statista.com/statistics/185334/number-of-bachelors-degrees-by-field-of-research/.

Oxford Languages, Version 12.4., s.v. "Entrepreneurship." : Oxford University Press, 2021 https://www.statista.com/statistics/185334/number-of-bachelors-degrees-by-field-of-research/.

Kelley, Donna. "The 582 Million Entrepreneurs in the World Are Not Created Equal." *The Hill*, March 12, 2017. *Entrepreneurship* 20, no. 2.3 (2018): 26-27. *Statista*, November 30, 2020. https://thehill.com/blogs/pundits-blog/economy-budget/323586-the-worlds-582-million-entrepreneurs-are-not-created-equal.

TEDx Talks. "TEDx Tucson George Lan the Failure of Success." February 16, 2011. Video, 13:06. https://twentyonetoys.com/blogs/teaching-21st-century-skills/creative-genius-divergent-thinking.

CHAPTER 1: THE ENTREPRENEURIAL MINDSET

Belsky, Scott. "Creativity Will Be Key To Competing Against AI In The Future Workforce-Here's How." *World Economic Forum*, November 10, 2020. https://www.weforum.org/agenda/2020/11/ai-automation-creativity-workforce-skill-fute-of-work/.

Franck, Thomas. "Post-Harvard Plans." *The Harvard Crimson*, 2017.
https://features.thecrimson.com/2017/senior-survey/after-harvard-narrative/index.html.

Hayes, Adam. "What is A Business." *Investopedia*, July 4, 2020.
https://www.investopedia.com/terms/b/business.asp.

NFTE. "Entrepreneurial Mindset." Accessed February 16, 2021.
https://www.nfte.com/entrepreneurial-mindset/#:~:text=What%20is%20an%20
Entrepreneurial%20Mindset,in%20a%20variety%20of%20settings.

Oxford Languages, Version 12.4., s.v. "Creativity." : Oxford University Press, 2021.
https://languages.oup.com/google-dictionary-en/.

Tamer, Mary. "On The Chopping Block, Again." *Harvard ED*, Summer 2009.
https://www.gse.harvard.edu/news/ed/09/06/chopping-block-again.

CHAPTER 2: WHAT IS CREATIVITY?

Anthony, Michelle. "Creative Development in 3-5 Year Olds." *Scholastic*, 2020.
https://www.scholastic.com/parents/family-life/creativity-and-critical-thinking/
development-milestones/creative-development-3-5-year-olds.html#:~:text=The%20
world%20of%20the%20preschooler,the%20developmental%20drive%20
towards%20conformity.

Brandt, Anthony and David Eagleman. "How Your Brain Takes Good Ideas
and Makes Them Better." *Psychology Today*, October 10, 2017. https://www.
psychologytoday.com/us/blog/the-guest-room/201710/how-your-brain-takes-good-
ideas-and-makes-them-better.

Florida, Richard. "*The Rise of the Creative Class: And How It's Transforming Work,
Leisure, Community, and Everyday Life.*" New York: Brilliance Audio, 2014.
https://www.amazon.com/Rise-Creative-Class-Transforming-Community/
dp/1469281422.

Hayes, John R. "Cognitive Process In Creativity." *Handbook Of Creativity*, (1989):135-145.
https://link.springer.com/chapter/10.1007%2F978-1-4757-5356-1_7.

IBM. "*IBM 2010 Global CEO Study: Creativity Selected as Most Crucial Factor for
Future Success.*" *IBM*, May 18, 2010.
https://www-03.ibm.com/press/us/en/pressrelease/31670.wss.

Kaufman, James and Ronald Beghetto. "Beyond Big And Little: The Four C Model
Of Creativity." *Sage Journals* 13, no. 1 (2009): 1-12.
https://journals.sagepub.com/doi/10.1037/a0013688.

Leveque, Lynne. *Breakthrough Creativity: Achieving Top Performance Using the
Eight Creative Talents.* Kansas City: Nicholas Brealey, 2011.
https://www.amazon.com/Breakthrough-Creativity-Achieving-Performance-
Creative-ebook/dp/B005Y94UMQ.

Novotney, Amy. "The Science of Creativity." *APA*, January 2009.
https://www.apa.org/gradpsych/2009/01/creativity.

Oxford Languages, Version 12.4., s.v. "Creativity." : Oxford University Press, 2021.
https://www.google.com/search?q=definition+of+creativity&oq=definition+of+crea
&aqs=chrome.0.69i59j69i57j0i433i457j0i131i433j0i433j0i131i433j0j0i433.2834j0j7&sour
ceid=chrome&ie=UTF-8.

Resnick, Mitch. "4 Myths About Creativity." *Edutopia*, November 20, 2017.
https://www.edutopia.org/article/4-myths-about-creativity.

Robinson, Ken. *Out of Our Minds: Learning to be Creative*. Westford, MA: Capstone, 2011.
https://www.amazon.com/Out-Our-Minds-Learning-Creative/dp/1907312471.

Wheeler Centre. "David Eagleman: The Creative Brain." May 28, 2018. Video, 1:04:50.
https://www.youtube.com/watch?v=8tN3J_V-J5w&ab_channel=WheelerCentre.

Winch, Guy. "10 Signs That You Might Have Fear Of Failure." *Psychology
Today*, June 18, 2013.
https://www.psychologytoday.com/us/blog/the-squeaky-wheel/201306/10-signs-
you-might-have-fear-failure.

CHAPTER 3: FIRST THINGS FIRST:
YOU DON'T HAVE TO BE A 'GENIUS'

About Facebook. "Company Info." Accessed January 29, 2021.
https://about.fb.com/company-info/.

Bhageria, Rajat. "An Interview With Seth Berkowitz | How the Founder of
Insomnia has Revolutionized The College Experience Armed Only With
Cookies." *HuffPost*, February 17, 2015.
https://www.huffpost.com/entry/an-interview-
with-seth-be_b_6638500?guccounter=1&guce_
referrer=aHR0cHM6Ly93d3cuZ29vZ2xlLmNvbS8S&guce_referrer_
sig=AQAAAIHaeQywTL6iqAlUk5vLw8LdgW_xDb_9WvvLKojxHBVIgZtm4-QLxJ
xBlNIufNVbgDMS3IMGUElPrYfz8k4vSlLiPzUL581P6kZYWevjjuSFBnj7QVdU2L9
ky24fXortRwSR39IMD640FkyZhffQUkXaplozpmuD6aF3nXgsT-v.

Clear, James. "Breaking Through Mental Blocks, Uncover Your Creative Genius,
and Make Brilliance a Habit." *Mastering Creativity* 1, (2014): 36.
https://jamesclear.com/wp-content/uploads/2014/10/creativity-v1.pdf.

Elkins, Kathleen and Taylor Rogers. "How Old 14 of the World's Richest People
Were When They First Became Billionaires." *Business Insider*, August 10, 2020.
https://www.businessinsider.com/how-old-billionaires-were-when-they-earned-
their-first-billion-2016-2#mark-zuckerberg-23-14.

Goodreads. "A Quote by Steve Jobs." Accessed January 29, 2021.
https://www.goodreads.com/quotes/653020-when-you-grow-up-you-tend-to-get-told-that-.

Oxford Languages, Version 12.4., s.v. "Genius." : Oxford University Press, 2021.
https://languages.oup.com/google-dictionary-en/.

Tarver, Evan. "Mark Zuckerberg Success Story: Net Worth, Education and
Influence." *Investopedia*, January 31, 2020.
https://www.investopedia.com/articles/personal-finance/081315/mark-zuckerberg-
success-story-net-worth-education-top-quotes.asp.

TEDx Talks. "TEDx Tucson George Lan the Failure of Success." February 16, 2011. Video, 13:06.
https://www.youtube.com/watch?v=ZfKMq-rYtnc.

Twenty One Toys. "Study Shows We are Born Creative Geniuses but the 'Education' System Dumbs Us Down." Accessed January 29, 2021.
https://twentyonetoys.com/blogs/teaching-21st-century-skills/creative-genius-divergent-thinking.

CHAPTER 4: THE ART OF BEING DISRUPTIVE

Arora, Priya. "Mindy Kaling's Netflix Show Tells a New Kind of Story: One Like Hers." *The New York Times*, April 27, 2020.
https://www.nytimes.com/2020/04/27/arts/television/mindy-kaling-never-have-I-ever-netflix.html.

CBS Sunday Morning. "Sunday Profile: Mindy Kaling." June 2, 2019. Video, 7:21.
https://www.youtube.com/watch?v=MgWLGW6rnvY&ab_channel=CBSSundayMorning.

Chen, Rosalie. "Here's how the CEO of Figma went from a computer science intern to the head of a $2 billion company that's challenging Adobe for the love of designers across Silicon Valley." *Business Insider*, October 1, 2020.
https://www.businessinsider.com/figma-ceo-dylan-field-design-software-startup-2020-10.

Dartmouth. "Dartmouth's 2018 Commencement Address by Mindy Kaling '01." June 10, 2018. Video, 17:02.
https://www.youtube.com/watch?v=JgUDjixWB5I.

Figma. "Back to School? Marc Andreessen says get clear-eyed on what your education will give you." August 12, 2020. Video, 58:37.
https://www.youtube.com/watch?v=_s1xyZM-2Gw&ab_channel=Figma.

Grant, Adam. Originals: How Non-Conformists Move the World. New York: the Penguin Books, 2017.
https://www.amazon.com/Originals-How-Non-Conformists-Move-World/dp/014312885X/ref=asc_df_014312885X/?tag=hyprod-20&linkCode=df0&hvadid=312243616995&hvpos=&hvnetw=g&hvrand=15191186411583150457&hvpone=&hvptwo=&hvqmt=&hvdev=c&hvdvcmdl=&hvlocint=&hvlocphy=9002065&hvtargid=pla-457258121964&psc=1.

Lang, Brent. "Mindy Kaling Created Her Own Opportunities (and Doesn't Plan on Stopping)." *Boston Herald*, January 23, 2019.
https://www.bostonherald.com/2019/01/23/mindy-kaling-created-her-own-opportunities-and-doesnt-plan-on-stopping/.

Mautz, Scott. "Science Says This Is Why You Fear Change(and What to Do About it.)" *Inc*, November 16, 2017.
https://www.inc.com/scott-mautz/science-says-this-is-why-you-fear-change-and-what-to-do-about-it.html.

Swift, Jackie. "How We Make Decisions and Take Risks." CornellResearch, November 7, 2019.
https://research.cornell.edu/news-features/how-we-make-decisions-and-take-risks.

The Paley Center for Media. "The Mindy Project - Mindy Kaling On The Show's Origins And Development." July 24, 2014. Video, 6:00. https://www.youtube.com/watch?v=NGV-izRrEPs.

theoffcamerashow. "Mindy Kaling shares her early experiences in 'The Office' writers room." October 5, 2016. Video, 2:56. https://www.youtube.com/watch?v=uY5_eoL7mjw&lc=UgjCJMWt9TcDhngCoAEC.

Twin, Alexandra. "Disruptive Innovation." *Investopedia*, February 22, 2021. https://www.investopedia.com/terms/d/disruptive-innovation.asp.

CHAPTER 5: MANIPULATE YOUR MOTIVATION

Bazigos, Michael and Emily Caruso. "Why Frontline Workers are Disengaged." McKinsey & Company, March 2, 2016. https://www.mckinsey.com/business-functions/organization/our-insights/why-frontline-workers-are-disengaged.

Ben & Jerry's. "About Us." Accessed January 31, 2021. https://www.benjerry.com/about-us.

National Scientific Council on the Developing Child. "Understanding Motivation: Building the Brain Architecture That Supports Learning, Health, and Community Participation." Center on the Developing Child, January 20, 2021. https://developingchild.harvard.edu/resources/understanding-motivation-building-the-brain-architecture-that-supports-learning-health-and-community-participation/.

Oxford Languages, Version 12.4, s.v. "Passion." : Oxford University Press, 2021. https://languages.oup.com/google-dictionary-en/.

Self Determination Theory. "Theory." Accessed February 28, 2021. https://selfdeterminationtheory.org/theory/.

Souders, Beata. "The Vital Importance and Benefits of Motivation." *Positive Psychology*, November 12, 2020. https://positivepsychology.com/benefits-motivation/#:~:text=Understanding%20motivation%20gives%20us%20many,fear%2C%20anger%2C%20and%20compassion.

Stillman, Cory. "Chef Movie True Story: How Much is Based on Jon Favreau's Real Life." *ScreenRant*, December 3, 2020. https://screenrant.com/chef-movie-true-story-jon-favreau-real-life/.

The Hollywood Reporter. "Jon Favreau & Roy Choi on Chef Inspiration: Rule Breakers." June 7, 2019. Video, 4:11. https://www.youtube.com/watch?v=3ZmXofWhpGM&ab_channel=TheHollywoodReporter.

CHAPTER 6: THE POWER OF PERSEVERANCE

Avatar The Last Airbender. "The Guru/The Crossroads of Destiny." Netflix. 47:00, December 1, 2006. https://www.netflix.com/watch/70136330?trackId=14277283&tctx=-97%2C-97%2C%2C%2C.

Baker, Brandon. "Infrequently Asked Questions: How does 2-D animation work?" *PhillyVoice*, April 5, 2017. https://hbr.org/2015/12/giving-up-is-the-enemy-of-creativity.

Dahl, Melissa. "Don't Believe the Hype About Grit, Pleads the Scientist Behind the Concept." *The Cut*, May 9, 2016. https://www.thecut.com/2016/05/dont-believe-the-hype-about-grit-pleads-the-scientist-behind-the-concept.html.

DeSteno, David. "The Connection Between Pride and Persistence." *HBR*, August 22, 2016. https://hbr.org/2016/08/the-connection-between-pride-and-persistence.

Dictionary.com, (Oxford: Lexico, 2008), s.v. "Genius is one percent inspiration and ninety-nine percent perspiration." https://www.dictionary.com/browse/genius-is-one-percent-inspiration-and-ninety-nine-percent-perspiration.

Nordgren, Loran and Brian Lucas. "Your Best Ideas Are Often Your Last Ideas." *HBR*, January 26, 2021 January 26, 2021. https://hbr.org/2021/01/your-best-ideas-are-often-your-last-ideas.

Porter, Rick. "'Avatar: Last Airbender' Expanded Universe Set at Nickelodeon." *The Hollywood Reporter*, February 24, 2021. https://www.hollywoodreporter.com/live-feed/avatar-last-airbender-expanded-universe-nickelodeon.

UltimateKorraTV. "Avatar: The Last Airbender Documentary (Full)- Avatar Spirits." May 18, 2013, Video, 32:19. https://www.youtube.com/watch?v=vdw6YmO8q_k&ab_channel=UltimateKorraTV.

CHAPTER 7: EMBRACING AUTHENTICITY

Almeida, Nicole. "Wholehearted Obsession: A Conversation With Finneas." *Atwood Magazines*, April 27, 2018. https://atwoodmagazine.com/finneas-2018-interview/.

AWAL. "SPACES: Inside the Tiny Bedroom Where FINNEAS and Billie Eilish Are Redefining Pop Music." April 2, 2019. Video, 5:00. https://www.youtube.com/watch?v=ZBJ914ha6LQ&ab_channel=AWAL.

Brannigan, Maura. "How Patagonia Keeps Its Brand Message Authentic In The Midst of An Activewear Boom." *Fashionista*, June 27, 2016 https://fashionista.com/2016/06/patagonia-activewear.

Cutler, R.J, director. 2021. *Billie Eilish: The World's A Little Blurry*. Production Neon Apple TV+. https://tv.apple.com/us/movie/billie-eilish-the-worlds-a-little-blurry/umc.cmc.5waz3hfo9r1133t8arap8b6nq.

Dove. "The 'Dove Real Beauty Pledge.'" Accessed March 18, 2021. https://www.dove.com/us/en/stories/about-dove/dove-real-beauty-pledge.html.

Fisher, Jennifer, "How Unilever's Dove Delivers on Its Brand Purpose." *The Wall Street Journal*, May 13, 2020. https://deloitte.wsj.com/cmo/2020/05/13/how-unilevers-dove-delivers-on-its-brand-purpose/.

Hull, Patrick. "It's Not All About The Money." *Forbes*, March 11, 2014. https://www.forbes.com/sites/patrickhull/2014/03/11/its-not-all-about-the-money/?sh=442e1b7a396c.

Hutchinson, Bryan. "Why You Are Not At Your Most Creative (And How To Be)."*Positive Writer*, Accessed March 18, 2021. http://positivewriter.com/why-you-are-not-at-your-most-creative-and-how-to-be/.

Lancer, Darlene. "The Power of Authenticity: 6 Steps to Achieve it." *Medium*, July 25, 2016. https://medium.com/becoming-you/the-power-of-authenticity-6-steps-to-achieve-it-a177aa513e41.

Noble, James. "Truth Will Out- Why Authenticity is the Key to Growing Your Business." *Neil Patel*, January 24, 2020. https://neilpatel.com/blog/truth-will-out/#:~:text=Simply%20put%2C%20being%20authentic%20means,Authenticity%20works%20because%E2%80%80%A6.

Pasricha, Neil. "The 3 A's of Awesome." (Lecture, TED, 2010) https://www.ted.com/talks/neil_pasricha_the_3_a_s_of_awesome.

Patagonia. "Core Values" Accessed March 18, 2021. https://www.patagonia.com/core-values/.

SiriusXM. "How Does Finneas Decide if a Song is for Him or for Billie Eilish." October 28, 2019. Video, 4:52. https://www.youtube.com/watch?v=EQ8HVGFGtCg&ab_channel=SiriusXM.

The Late Late Show With James Corden. "Billie Eilish Carpool Karaoke." December 20, 2019. Video, 17:04. https://www.youtube.com/watch?v=uh2qGWfmESk&ab_channel=TheLateLateShowwithJamesCorden.

Wood, Alex Mathew, P. Alex Linley, John Maltby and Michael Baliousi. "The Authentic Personality: A Theoretical and Empirical Conceptualization and the Development of the Authenticity Scale." *ResearchGate*, July 2008. https://www.researchgate.net/publication/42739517_The_Authentic_Personality_A_Theoretical_and_Empirical_Conceptualization_and_the_Development_of_the_Authenticity_Scale.

CHAPTER 8: CREATING YOU OWN LUCK

Acton, Michael. "Calm Co-founder: Michael Acton Smith a Pioneer in Mental Health and Wellness." October 26, 2020. *Stigma* by Stephen Hays. Podcast audio, 18:46. https://stigmapodcast.com/calm-co-founder-michael-acton-smith-a-pioneer-in-mental-health-and-wellness/#:~:text=Calm%20origin%20story%3A%20With%20his,mental%20health%20for%20the%20better.

Calm. "Michael Acton Smith OBE." Accessed March 18, 2021. https://blog.calm.com/michael-acton-smith.

Lagorio-Chafkin, Christine. "Michael Acton Smith's 'Completely Bonkers' Journey to Founding Calm, a Wellness App With a $1Billion Valuation." *Inc*, October 14, 2019. https://www.inc.com/christine-lagorio-chafkin/michael-acton-smith-calm-2019-inc-5000-conference.html.

Oppong, Thomas. "Ideas Are Everywhere: The Best Clues for Spotting Business Ideas." *AllTopStartups*, February 5, 2015. https://alltopstartups.com/2015/02/05/spotting-business-ideas/.

Oxford Languages, Version 12.4, s.v. "Visionary." : Oxford University Press, 2021. https://www.google.com/search?q=meaning+for+visionary&rlz=1C5CHFA_enUS862US866&oq=meaning+for+visionary&aqs=chrome..69i57j0l5.4368j1j9&sourceid=chrome&ie=UTF-8.

Pinola, Melanie. "'Luck Is What Happens When Preparation Meets Opportunity.'" *LifeHacker*, July 19, 2013. https://lifehacker.com/luck-is-what-happens-when-preparation-meets-opportunit-821189862.

Jacobs, John and Bert Jacobs "The Life Is Good Company: Bert and John Jacobs." September 2, 2019. *How I Built this With Guy Raz* by Guy Raz. Podcast audio, 63:00. https://www.npr.org/2019/08/30/755877251/the-life-is-good-company-bert-and-john-jacobs.

Shapiro, Gary. *Ninja Innovation: The Ten Killer Strategies of the World's Most Successful Businesses.* New York: HarperCollins Publishers, 2015. https://www.amazon.com/Ninja-Innovation-Strategies-Successful-Businesses/dp/0062242334.

Thompson, John. "The World Of The Entrepreneur - A New Perspective." *Journal of Workplace Learning* 11, No. 6(1999): 209-224. https://www.emerald.com/insight/content/doi/10.1108/13665629910284990/full/html#idm46415736932080.

Walters, Natalie. "The Fascinating Story of How 2 Brother Went From Running A Failing Business Out of a Van to Building a $130 million Company." *Business Insider*, April 16, 2017. https://www.businessinsider.com/the-success-story-of-life-is-good-2016-2.

Zeitchik, Steven. "Hollywood wants to put you to sleep." *The Washington Post*, November 2, 2020. https://www.washingtonpost.com/business/2020/11/02/calming-entertainment-in-tense-times/.

CHAPTER 9: GO TOGETHER & GO FAR

Beattie, Andrew. "Steve Jobs and the Apple Story." *Investopedia*, March 14, 2020. https://www.investopedia.com/articles/fundamental-analysis/12/steve-jobs-apple-story.asp.

Darrisaw, Michelle. "How These Furloughed Sisters Used the Government Shutdown to Launch a Cheesecake Business." *Oprah Magazine*, July 31, 2019. https://www.oprahmag.com/life/work-money/a26088711/furlough-cheesecake-company-sisters-interview/.

Fabry, Merrill. "Ben & Jerry's Is Turning 40. Here's How They Captured a Trend That Changed American Ice Cream." *Time*, May 4, 2018. https://time.com/5252406/ben-jerry-ice-cream-40/https://time.com/5252406/ben-jerry-ice-cream-40/.

Hitt, Caitlyn. "The Ice Cream- and Activism- Filled History of Ben & Jerry's." *Thrillist*, August 12, 2020. https://www.thrillist.com/news/nation/the-history-of-ben-jerrys-ice-cream.

Howard, Nikki and Jaqi Wright. "Cheesecake Business Born During Shutdown Hits Walmart." June 30, 2019. *Business* by Michael Martin. Podcast audio, 2:00. https://www.npr.org/2019/06/30/737478300/cheesecake-business-born-during-shutdown-hits-walmart.

Larkin, Martina and Derek O'Halloran. "Collaboration Between Start-ups and Corporates." World Economic Forum (2018): 1-21. http://www3.weforum.org/docs/WEF_White_Paper_Collaboration_between_Start-ups_and_Corporates.pdf.

Marchese, David. "Ben & Jerry's Radical Ice Cream Dreams." *The New York Times*, July 27, 2020. https://www.nytimes.com/interactive/2020/07/27/magazine/ben-jerry-interview.html.

Marosz, Jonathan, narrator. "Group Genius: The Creative Power of Collaboration." Keith Sawyer (audiobook). January 14, 2008. Accessed January 31, 2021. https://www.amazon.com/Group-Genius-Keith-Sawyer-audiobook/dp/B0012OMFAG/ref=sr_1_1?dchild=1&keywords=Group+Genius&qid=1612055644&s=books&sr=1-1 .

NASA. "The Wright Brothers' Story." Accessed January 31, 2021. https://www.nasa.gov/audience/foreducators/k-4/features/F_Wright_Brothers_Story.html.

Satell, Greg. *Mapping Innovation: A Playbook for Navigating a Disruptive Age*. New York: McGraw Hill Education, 2017. https://www.amazon.com/Mapping-Innovation-Playbook-Navigating-Disruptive/dp/1259862259.

Taggar, Harj. "How to Find the Right Co-Founder." Y Combinator, November 2, 2020.

"Reason Teamwork is Important In The Workplace." YTI, March 26, 2015. https://www.ycombinator.com/library/8h-how-to-find-the-right-co-founder.

CHAPTER 10: WHAT WOULD AN ENTERTAINER DO?

Boris, Vanessa. "What Makes Storytelling So Effective for Learning." *Harvard Business Publishing*, December 20, 2017. https://www.harvardbusiness.org/what-makes-storytelling-so-effective-for-learning/#:~:text=Telling%20stories%20is%20one%20of,and%20values%20that%20unite%20people.

Disney Plus. "The Imagineering Story." November 12, 2019. Video, 69:00.
https://www.disneyplus.com/series/the-imagineering-story/6ryoXv1e1rWW.

James, Michelle. "The New Storytellers: Michelle James." November 25, 2018.
Storytelling and the Creative Process by Michael Margols. Podcast audio, .
https://www.getstoried.com/storytelling-and-the-creative-process/.

Michael Giacchino. "Michael Giacchino." Accessed January 30, 2021.
https://michaelgiacchino.com/biography/#:~:text=Giacchino%20was%20the%20
musical%20director,picture%20with%20a%20full%20orchestra.

Myint, Ba. "George Lucas and the Origin Story Behind 'Star Wars'." *Biography*,
October 14, 2020.
https://www.biography.com/news/george-lucas-star-wars-facts.

O'Hara, Helen. "Film Studies 101: Michael Giacchino On Being A Composer."
Empire Online, May 30, 2014.
https://www.empireonline.com/movies/features/film-studies-101-michael-
giacchino-composer/.

Pixar Post. "Incredibles 2 Scoring Session B-Roll & Michael Giacchino & Brad Bird
Interview." June 7, 2018. Video, 4:46.
https://www.youtube.com/watch?v=WQkfwsuzAOs&ab_channel=PixarPost.

CHAPTER 11: PATIENCE IS YOUR PAL

Blakely, Sara. "How Spanx Got Started." *Inc*, January 20, 2012.
https://www.inc.com/sara-blakely/how-sara-blakley-started-spanx.html.

Jones, Christopher. "Patience is the Unsung Hero of Creativity." *Christopher P Jones*,
May 10, 2019.
https://christopherpjones.medium.com/patience-is-the-unsung-hero-of-creativity-
944a44796c37.

Long, Jonathan. "Starting A Business Does Not Mean You're Your Own Boss, and Other
Misconceptions About Being An Entrepreneur." *Business Insider*, October 8, 2015.
https://www.businessinsider.com/12-common-misconceptions-about-being-an-
entrepreneur-2015-10.

MasterClass. "MasterClass Live with Sara Blakely." June 18, 2020. Video, 1:01:37.
https://www.youtube.com/watch?v=ml35J1s0gCI.

Orloff, Judith. "The Power of Patience." *Psychology Today*, September 18, 2012.
https://www.psychologytoday.com/us/blog/emotional-freedom/201209/the-power-
patience#:~:text=Practicing%20patience%20will%20help%20you,of%20your%20
life%20will%20improve.

Segal, Gillian. "This Self- Made Billionaire Failed The LSAT Twice, Then Sold
Fax Machines For 7 Years Before Hitting Big—Here's How She Got There." *CNBC*,
April 3, 2019.
https://www.cnbc.com/2019/04/03/self-made-billionaire-spanx-founder-sara-
blakely-sold-fax-machines-before-making-it-big.html#:~:text=In%202012%2C%20
Spanx%20founder%20Sara,according%20to%20the%20publication's%20estimates.

CHAPTER 12: BELIEVE & YOU'RE HALFWAY THERE

Bandura, Albert. *Self-Efficacy Mechanism in Human Agency* Volume 37, no. 2 (1982): 122-147.
https://www.uky.edu/~eushe2/Bandura/Bandura1982AP.pdf.

Chobani. "Hamdi Ulukaya, Chobani Founder's Story." April 8, 2013. Video, 1:32.
https://www.youtube.com/watch?v=578FODRPRa0&ab_channel=Chobani.

Churchill, Winston. "Attitude is A Little Thing That Makes a Big Difference."
BrainyQuote, Accessed January 31, 2020.
https://www.brainyquote.com/quotes/winston_churchill_104164.

OMAR ELATTAR & THE PASSIONATE FE. "Janitor Who Created Hot Cheetos:
Amazing Life Story Interview! (Must Watch)." October 6, 2017. Video, 1:42:10.
https://www.youtube.com/watch?v=ADnYF7srPK0.

Ulukaya, Hamdi. "The Anti-CEO Playbook." (Lecture, TED, 2019).
https://www.ted.com/talks/hamdi_ulukaya_the_anti_ceo_playbook/
transcript?language=en#t-14121.

Whalen, Andrew. "The True Story OF the Flamin' Hot Cheetos Inventor Richard
Montañez." *Newsweek*, August 27, 2019.
https://www.newsweek.com/flamin-hot-cheeto-movie-true-story-creator-
richard-montanez-1456377#:~:text=In%201976%20%E2%80%94%20
Monta%C3%B1ez%20was%2018,plant%20in%20Rancho%20Cucamonga%2C%20
California.&text=Monta%C3%B1ez%20invented%20the%20Flamin'%20
Hot,without%20the%20cheese%20powder%20dust.

CHAPTER 13: REFLECT SO YOU DON'T REPEAT

Gibson, Kelsie. "Looking Back Now, Taylor Swift Wouldn't Give Her Younger Self
Any Advice." *Popsugar*, December 13, 2019.
https://www.popsugar.com/celebrity/taylor-swift-quotes-in-billboard-women-in-
music-2019-issue-47002958.

Perkins, Melanie. "21 Questions from Aussie Startups: Highs, Lows & Lessons
learned during Canva's Journey So Far." *LinkedIn*, January 16, 2018.
https://www.linkedin.com/pulse/21-questions-from-aussie-startups-highs-lows-
lessons-learned-perkins/.

Porter, Jennifer. "Why You Should Make Time for Self-Reflection (Even If You Hate
Doing It)." *HBR*, March 21, 2017.
https://hbr.org/2017/03/why-you-should-make-time-for-self-reflection-even-if-you-
hate-doing-it#:~:text=The%20most%20useful%20reflection%20involves,possible%20
interpretations%2C%20and%20create%20meaning.

Putra, Yogi. "What I Learned from Steve Jobs' Connecting The Dots." *Medium*,
April 4, 2019.
https://medium.com/@yogiariefputra/what-i-learn-from-steve-jobs-connecting-
the-dots-8ca0397cffe1.

Stanford "Steve Jobs' 2005 Stanford Commencement Address." March 7, 2008. Video, 15:04.
https://www.youtube.com/watch?v=UF8uR6Z6KLc.

Wilson, Lana, director. *Miss Americana*. Netflix Original Film, 2020.
https://www.netflix.com/title/81028336.

CHAPTER 14: THINK CREATIVITY, NOT PRODUCTIVITY

Almendrala, Anna. "Lin-Manuel Miranda It's 'No Accident' Hamilton Came To Me On Vacation." *Landit*, May 26, 2018.
https://landit.com/articles/lin-manuel-miranda-its-no-accident-hamilton-came-to-me-on-vacation.

Gilbert, Daniel. *Stumbling on Happiness*. New York: Alfred A. Knopf, 2007.
https://www.amazon.com/Stumbling-Happiness-Daniel-Gilbert/dp/1400077427.

Gollwitzer, Peter. *The Psychology of Action: Link Cognition and Motivation to Behavior*. New York: The Guilford Press, 1996.
https://www.amazon.com/Psychology-Action-Cognition-Motivation-Behavior/dp/1572300329.

Malone-Kircher, Madison. "James Dyson on 5,126 Vacuums That Didn't Work-and the One That Finally Did." *New York Magazine*, November 16, 2016.
https://nymag.com/vindicated/2016/11/james-dyson-on-5-126-vacuums-that-didnt-work-and-1-that-did.html.

Newport, Cal. *Deep Work*. New York: Grand Central Publishing, 2016.
https://www.amazon.com/Deep-Work-Focused-Success-Distracted/dp/1455586692.

Oxford Languages, Version 12.4., s.v. "Productivity." : Oxford University Press, 2021.
https://languages.oup.com/google-dictionary-en/.

Parekh, Rupal. "Global Study: 75% Of People Think They're Not Living Up To Creative Potential." *Ad Age*, April 23, 2012.
https://adage.com/article/news/study-75-living-creative-potential/234302.

Roberto, Michael. *Unlocking Creativity*. New Jersey: John Wiley & Sons, 2019.
https://www.amazon.com/Unlocking-Creativity-Solve-Problem-Decisions/dp/111954579X.

Robinson, Adam. "Want to Boost Your Bottom Line? Encourage Your Employees to Work on Side Projects." *Inc*, March 12, 2018.
https://www.inc.com/adam-robinson/google-employees-dedicate-20-percent-of-their-time-to-side-projects-heres-how-it-works.html.

Scalco, Dan. "23 Powerful Quotes to Get Your Creativity Flowing." *Inc*, January 23, 2018.
https://www.inc.com/dan-scalco/23-powerful-quotes-to-get-your-creativity-flowing.html.

Vanderkam, Laura. *What the Most Successful People Do at Work: A Short Guide to Making Over Your Career*. New York: the Penguin Group, 2013.
https://www.amazon.com/What-Most-Successful-People-Work-ebook/dp/B00BPDR4BY.

Zomorodi, Manoush. *Bored and Brilliant: How Spacing Out Can Unlock Your Most Productive and Creative Self.* New York: St. Martin's Press, 2017. https://www.amazon.com/Bored-Brilliant-Spacing-Productive-Creative/dp/1250124956.

CHAPTER 15: IF YOU DON'T KNOW, HAVE A GO

Bandura, Albert, Edward Blanchard and Brunhilde Ritter. "Relative Efficacy of Desensitization and Modeling Approaches For Inducing Behavioral, Affective, and Attitudinal Changes." *Journal of Personality and Social Psychology* 13, No. 3 (1969): 173-199. http://www.uky.edu/~eushe2/Bandura/Bandura1969JPSP.pdf.

Bryant, Sean. "How Many Startups Fail and Why?" *Investopedia*, November 9, 2020.

Freudenrich, Craig and Robynne Boyd. "How Your Brain Works." Howstuffworks, June 25, 2020. https://www.investopedia.com/articles/personal-finance/040915/how-many-startups-fail-and-why.asp#:~:text=The%20Bottom%20Line,succeed%20in%20the%20first%20year.

Kelley, Tom and David Kelley. *Creative Confidence: Unleashing the Creative Potential Within Us All.* New York: Crown Publishing, 2013. https://www.amazon.com/Creative-Confidence-Unleashing-Potential-Within/dp/038534936X.

Popoava, Maria. "The Importance of Frustration in the Creative Process Animated." *Brain Pickings*, November 2, 2015. https://www.brainpickings.org/2012/03/26/flash-rosenberg-jonah-lehrer-imagine/.

Stillman, Jessica. "Stacey Abrams Has 5 Powerful Words for Anyone Who Thinks They Aren't Cut Out for Success." *Inc*, January 6, 2021. https://www.inc.com/jessica-stillman/stacey-abrams-sheryl-sandberg-success-lesson.html.

Walton, Alice. "7 Assumptions Smart People Never Make." *Forbes*, May 31, 2014. https://www.forbes.com/sites/alicegwalton/2014/01/24/7-bad-habits-assumptions-that-successful-people/?sh=1bc92e2744f5.

CHAPTER 16: WHY NOW?

Anthony, Michelle. "Creative Development in 3-5 Year Olds." *Scholastic*, 2020. https://www.scholastic.com/parents/family-life/creativity-and-critical-thinking/development-milestones/creative-development-3-5-year-olds.html#:~:text=The%20world%20of%20the%20preschooler,the%20developmental%20drive%20towards%20conformity.

Florida, Richard. "*The Rise of the Creative Class: And How It's Transforming Work, Leisure, Community, and Everyday Life.*" New York: Brilliance Audio, 2014. https://www.amazon.com/Rise-Creative-Class-Transforming-Community/dp/1469281422.

IBM. "*IBM 2010 Global CEO Study: Creativity Selected as Most Crucial Factor for Future Success.*" IBM, May 18, 2010. https://www-03.ibm.com/press/us/en/pressrelease/31670.wss.

Leveque, Lynne. *Breakthrough Creativity: Achieving Top Performance Using the Eight Creative Talents*. Kansas City: Nicholas Brealey, 2011. https://www.amazon.com/Breakthrough-Creativity-Achieving-Performance-Creative-ebook/dp/B005Y94UMQ.

Robinson, Ken. *Out of Our Minds: Learning to be Creative*. Westford, MA: Capstone, 2011. https://www.amazon.com/Out-Our-Minds-Learning-Creative/dp/1907312471.